Ronald Reagan

Ronald Reagan

✦

From Sports to Movies to Politics

Libby Hughes

iUniverse, Inc.
New York Lincoln Shanghai

Ronald Reagan
From Sports to Movies to Politics

Copyright © 2005 by Libby Hughes

iUniverse books may be ordered through booksellers or by contacting:

iUniverse
2021 Pine Lake Road, Suite 100
Lincoln, NE 68512
www.iuniverse.com
1-800-Authors (1-800-288-4677)

Interior photo credits: Libby Hughes; Ronald Reagan Presidential Library

ISBN: 0-595-33658-2

Printed in the United States of America

Dedicated to five special young people:
Mary Ellen, Amanda, Rebecca, Abbie, John Lloyd,
and their parents

Contents

ACKNOWLEDGMENTS

Georgia Dearborn, Janet Koehler, Tom Wilson, Pam Van Kirk, Marilyn Jones, Grace Jackson, Joan Smutny, Amy and Lloyd McElhiney, Art and Marge Wetzell, Marilyn and Ted Trulock, Maxine Gaumer, Tony Glass, Mindy Hartman, Nancy Rutherford, Susan Trevor, Yvonne Knapp, Mayor John Reitman, Mayor Jim Burke, Bill Thompson, Mark Minnick, Jim Zabel, Sherry Fletcher, Joy Hodges, Doris Fields Heller, Carol Ann Ross, Betsy M. Zavell, Kathryn Field, Betsey Welton, Ernie Silva, Marian Carlson, Jack B. Lindsey.

Preface

Research for an author has expanded by the wonders and resources of the internet. A writer can sit in front of a computer screen and write a complete biography without ever stepping outside.

However, this is unacceptable for me as a biographer. There is no substitute for on-the-ground research. After going into seclusion to read everything I possibly could about Ronald Reagan, I then packed my small van camper with my two Rhodesian Ridgeback dogs and began an 8,000 mile journey to discover the towns, homes, schools, and people connected to Ronald Reagan for my primary sources. My nationwide travels took me to six towns in Illinois, two cities in Iowa, and to the vast hills and desert of California, including the 153,000 square foot Ronald Reagan Presidential Library in Simi Valley, California. Seeing, feeling, and tasting the sights in person put flesh and bones on written descriptions. Interviewing people in each place helped to paint a fuller portrait of Reagan. The readers KNOW you have been there.

This plan of attack is nothing new for me. Having written ten biographies about international leaders and celebrities from Margaret Thatcher to Nelson Mandela to Tiger Woods, I know what is required in doing extensive research on each subject. For example, I drove 13,000 miles in pursuit of research relevant to Tiger Woods. For Nelson Mandela, I drove all over South Africa and met him in his home after his release from over 27 years in prison. For the book on Benazir Bhutto, I traveled extensively in Pakistan and interviewed Bhutto herself as well as people in London and at Harvard University.

As the wife of the State Department Spokesman during the first term of Ronald Reagan's presidency from 1981–1984 in Washington, D. C., I had the privilege of witnessing firsthand the inner workings of the Reagan administration. One time when I was at the White House for a social function, I greeted President Reagan in a receiving line and asked him how his vacation was. He and Mrs. Reagan had just returned from their ranch in California. The president stopped the entire line to tell me in detail about the vacation at his ranch. He would have done the same for anyone who had asked him that question. He was a people person.

How did this poor, but happy boy become the fortieth president?

Libby Hughes

Cape Cod and Cambridge, Massachusetts
December 2004

1

Born to Communicate

Two extraordinary people were born in 1911. They were Ronald Reagan and Ginger Rogers, the dancer/singer/actress. Reagan and Rogers would meet in Hollywood to star together in a 1950 movie called *Storm Warning.* In the 1980s President Reagan would invite Ginger Rogers to visit the White House several times. They both made their mark on the world: Reagan in movies and politics, Rogers on stage and in the film industry.

In the world at large, events seesawed between tragedy and hope in 1911. There were severe earthquakes in Russia and California. Millions of Chinese were starving from crop failure, but China would recover to become a republic in 1912. The Russians and Germans planned to build a railroad to transport oil from Baghdad, Iraq, to Berlin, Germany. By the end of 1911, the Norwegian explorer, Roald Amundsen, fought bitter cold weather and boulders of ice to reach the South Pole with his dog team.

Meanwhile, in a tiny town of 820 people in Tampico, Illinois, a momentous event was soon to happen in the apartment of a young family. Tampico sits alone in the heartland of America. Even today, Tampico is in the middle of flat, farming plains in the northwest section of Illinois. If you stand in the center of the one block of shops on Main Street and look up and down, the road stretches as far as you can see, disappearing into the pancake horizon. Because of this terrain, the town is vulnerable to spinning tornadoes in summer and ruthless snowstorms in winter. Even the town's newspaper in 1911, *The Tampico Tornado,* was an appropriate name, but such hardships drew the churches and community together.

During the first decade or two of the twentieth century, Tampico's main street was just a dirt road where horses, wagons, and a few cars were parked diagonally in front of shops and the bank. Corn, cattle, and pigs were the staples of farming and trade.

On a cold, February night in 1911, one of those memorable blizzards ripped across the open plains of Tampico, depositing mountains of drifting snow outside the storefronts. Early the next morning of February 6, everything was silent. Everything was white. The people of Tampico were asleep. Only one small lamp burned in an apartment over the bakery below—in 1919 the bakery became a bank. The sweet smells of cookies and homemade bread filled the empty street and Reagan apartment. Nelle Wilson Reagan labored to deliver her second child. Although Dr. H. A. Terry was staying with friends only a few doors down from the Reagans, he had to fight the barricades of snowdrifts to reach the door going upstairs into the five-room apartment. Once there, he hurried into the front bedroom, overlooking the silent street below, to attend Mrs. Reagan, assisted by her midwife.

Between four and six in the morning of February 6, 1911, a ten-pound baby boy filled the bedroom with his healthy cries. "The Great Communicator"—as he would become known— was already speaking his mind. This newborn baby was Ronald Wilson Reagan. His father, John (Jack) Edward Reagan, raced across the street from his store, leapt up the stairs, and burst into the room to see his new son. With a twinkle in his eye, he laughed and said, "He looks like a fat little Dutchman. But who knows, he might some day become President!" That was a humorous remark, which eventually would come true.

Two-year-old Neil Reagan stared at his new brother and said, "I wanted a sister, not a loud crying brother!"

Nelle Reagan looked adoringly at her newborn and said, "He's wonderful."

Jack Reagan felt like a proud new father. When he opened the H. C. Pitney general dry goods store across the street, he celebrated by giving his customers extra yardage of material for free.

One lady asked, "How's your new baby, Mr. Reagan?"

"Fat and noisy. He weighs ten pounds and looks like a fat, little Dutchman," he replied. They both smiled.

Throughout his son's childhood, Jack called him "the Dutchman." Ronald Reagan never liked his first name and eventually decided to take the nickname of "Dutch." It stuck. Everyone from his youth, except his mother Nelle, called him Dutch Reagan. The name traveled with him through much of his lifetime.

During the first three months that the Reagans lived in their apartment above the bakery, they had to heat their home by coal, stored out back. The outhouse was also behind the building as was the pump for supplying water. The stairs up and down were steep. The rent was ten dollars or less a month, paid by Jack's salary of a dollar a day. Whenever Nelle wanted to go out shopping, she would go to the back screen porch, knock on her neighbor's window, and hand little Ronald Reagan to her for baby-sitting. Nelle and her neighbor, who had a baby girl, would take turns baby-sitting. The long porch was the place where Nelle washed the family clothes in a big tub with a washboard, except in winter.

Nelle and Jack managed to have a social life as well. They were active performers in amateur productions at the Opera House, which is now torn down. A couple of blocks away, Nelle attended and did good works at the Church of Christ, visiting the sick and needy.

Tampico held cherished boyhood memories for Ronald Reagan. The family lived there twice. They stayed the first time until Mr. Pitney sold his store. Dutch was almost four by then. They returned when Dutch was nine. Those toddler years were filled with typical child's play. Jack Reagan, fascinated by the new automobiles being made in the 1900s, decided to build Dutch a wooden car that he could sit in and drive with pedals for his third birthday. At the same time, he gave his son his first American flag, which he waved while pedaling the little car around the block. Patriotism began early for the Reagan youngster.

Dutch followed brother Neil everywhere. Often Neil was a mischief-maker. They climbed over the Civil War cannon and pyramid of cannon balls on the green lawn of Memorial Park, facing their white Victorian house on Glassburn Street. The Reagans had moved there when Dutch was three months old. Across the park were the railroad tracks. One hot summer's afternoon, Neil spotted an ice wagon on the other side of a train that had just arrived.

"Come on, Dutch, let's get some ice chips," said Neil.

"Okay," Dutch replied in that husky voice of his.

The two boys ran from their house to the train and squeezed under one of the railroad cars. They each grabbed a fist full of ice and started sucking them. Then, they wiggled back under the train just as it jerked forward. The boys stepped out of a cloud of steam as the train started to move. At that very moment, their mother looked out the window and saw her boys. She realized they could have been crushed by the train and raced to them across the park. She dragged them home by grabbing each boy by an ear. Once inside the Victorian house, she spanked them.

Ronald Reagan recalled the incident and said that he and his brother received "the appropriate punishment."

2

Two Parents and Two Religions

Nelle and Jack Reagan had fallen in love in Fulton, Illinois, just south of Tampico. Many residents came from Holland to settle there where they raised their chubby babies. Nelle and Jack had met in a department store where they both had worked. Jack was a handsome Irishman with relatives from County Tipperary in Ireland. He was full of stories to tell his shy girl friend, who twinkled and laughed at his jokes. The petite, pretty Nelle Wilson was of Scots/English background. She was a twenty-year-old Protestant and he was a twenty-one-year-old Catholic. He was more of a pessimist and she was definitely an optimist. Nelle always saw the best in people and if anything bad happened, she was sure the future held a better plan. Though a pair of opposites, they made a fine looking couple and married in 1904.

Jack Reagan had a brother, but they somehow had lost contact with each other. Nelle had five sisters and brothers. The Reagans often visited some of the sisters: especially one that lived in Quincy, Illinois. Another ran a hotel in the Ozark Mountains of Arkansas while still another lived in Morrison, Illinois.

Neither of Ronald Reagan's parents had gone beyond grade school, but Nelle loved to read and taught her sons to appreciate books. She also loved the theatre and gave readings at her church or at social gatherings. In those days, it was the fashion to memorize poems or plays or speeches and present them before a church or local audience. Sometimes Nelle and Jack would entertain their friends. He would tell stories or they would perform together.

Nelle tried to involve her sons in these dramatic readings. Dutch was more reluctant than Neil, who was an extrovert like his father. He had no hesitation in drawing attention to himself. Both boys were raised in different churches and religions. Jack and Neil Reagan were baptized in the Catholic Church while Dutch followed his mother's religion, Disciples of Christ from the First Christian Church. Their loyalties would remain in these separate denominations throughout their lives.

Ronald Reagan's parents came from very different backgrounds. Jack was orphaned at the age of six when both his parents died of tuberculosis. An elderly aunt took him to live with her and made sure he went to the Catholic Church. In those days, prejudice against Irish Catholics was as strong as against blacks.

The attitude against Catholics gradually changed. However, while the Reagan boys were growing up in Illinois, there were very few Catholics. Their peers teased them for being Irish and Catholic, even though Dutch and his mother were Protestants. Many times, Dutch had to engage in fistfights to defend his family. Whatever the reasons for the brawls, Nelle and Jack would interfere to stop the fights. Secretly, Jack wanted his sons to win those fights, but he and Nelle insisted that their sons should not show prejudice to blacks or Jews.

"I remember when my father was on a business trip and a hotel manager refused to accommodate Jews. So strongly did my father feel that he turned around and left the hotel. He slept in his car for the night during a terrible snowstorm," recalled

Ronald Reagan. "We were encouraged to bring our black friends home from school for a meal or to spend the night with us if hotels wouldn't accept them."

Even though Jack Reagan was Irish, his patriotism for America was never in question. In fact, his greatest disappointment was his rejection by the Army in 1917 when America sent troops to Europe to support Great Britain and France in World War I. Because he was the father of two children, the Army denied his request to join.

World War I began in 1914 when a Serb assassinated the Archduke of Austria. Germany leapt into the war to stop Serbia from expanding into its territory. Then Germany invaded Belgium and France. Great Britain came to France's defense. The war officially ended on November 11, 1918, now called Armistice Day or Veteran's Day, which still remains a holiday in the twenty-first century.

"My mother and father took us to the railroad stations in Galesburg and Monmouth, Illinois, where we lived, to welcome the soldiers returning home,"

Reagan remembered. "We all had American flags and cheered."

In his autobiography Ronald Reagan said, "I learned from my father the value of hard work and ambition, and maybe a little something about telling a story. From my mother, I learned the value of prayer, how to have dreams and believe I could make them come true."

3

Moving from Town to Town

The Reagans were like a family of gypsies. They never stayed in one place too long. From 1914 to 1920 the Reagans would crisscross the state of Illinois, moving from town to town and house to house, following Jack Reagan and his many jobs. The frequent changes in schools and friends made Dutch very cautious in making lasting friendships for fear of a sudden move. This may explain why the adult Reagan was described as aloof—not making close friendships, except for his wife.

Within the above time frame, Woodrow Wilson would become president. In 1913 Cecil B. DeMille launched the film industry in Hollywood—an event that would affect Ronald Reagan's future. Albert Einstein discovered the Theory of Relativity in 1915. Germany provoked World War I from 1914 to 1917. In 1917 the Russian Revolution overthrew the czars. American women would earn the right to vote by 1920.

After Jack Reagan's boss, Mr. Pitney, decided to sell his store in Tampico, Jack Reagan was forced to look for a new job and found one at the Fair department store in Chicago in December 1914. He moved his family into an Irish Catholic neighborhood where he found a large second floor apartment in a yellow brick, three-story building at 832E 57th Street, close to the

University of Chicago in the Hyde Park section and close to his work at 67th Street.

Shortly after their arrival, four-year-old Dutch contracted bronchial pneumonia and was confined to his bed. A sympathetic neighbor brought him some lead soldiers to play with on the cover of the bed. He loved playing war with the soldiers and affectionately cherished memories of those lead toy soldiers as an adult. Soon he was well enough to stand in the corner bay window, watching horse-drawn fire engines speed down Cottage Grove, blaring their sirens. Like many a young boy, he wanted to be a fireman when he grew up.

In that busy neighborhood, brother Neil was sent to the butcher shop by his mother to buy liver and soup bones. He told the butcher that the liver was for their cat, which they never owned. On Sunday the family, not the imaginary cat, ate the liver for their main meal. They had stew and soup the rest of the week. As an adult, Reagan never liked liver, but he always loved macaroni and cheese. Other times, Nelle would mix oatmeal and hamburger into patties and soak them in gravy. The boys never realized they were poor. Their meals were tasty, especially the oatmeal patties. Ronald Reagan recalled them with a sense of nostalgia. To further enhance their income, Nelle would repair clothes for friends and neighbors. A sewing machine was always in the parlor or in the master bedroom of their many rental homes and apartments.

Nelle wasn't happy about living in the city with two small boys. Large, green Washington Park was only a few blocks away, but Cottage Grove was too busy a street to cross for her sons. At the end of 1915, Nelle was relieved when Jack Reagan found a job in the charming, historic city of Galesburg, Illinois, over one hundred miles west of Chicago. Much bigger than Tampico, Galesburg was the headquarters for a brick works factory. Also, the Ferris family invented the Ferris Wheel there. Galesburg was the birthplace of Carl Sandburg, Charles Walgreen of Walgreen Drugstore, and popcorn, which Nelle loved as a snack for her family. Located in the center of the city, Knox College was the site where Abraham Lincoln and Stephen A. Douglas debated outside the campus doors in 1858. Humorously, Lincoln climbed through a window at Knox College to show that he had been through college.

By a strange coincidence, Nancy Davis, Ronald Reagan's future wife, spent summers in Galesburg with her parents and grandparents. Her stepfather, Dr. Loyal Davis, had grown up in Galesburg, graduating from high school and Knox College before studying medicine in Chicago. These were happy times for Nancy. The owner of a grocery store had built a walk-in dollhouse for her. She also rode a pony during vacations in Galesburg. Since Ronald Reagan was ten years older than his wife-to-be, he wouldn't discover this connection until much later.

4

Discovering Butterflies and Words

Galesburg was a railroad center for Chicago and also a central point between the east and west coasts. The sound of trains thundered through the town day and night. The residents were so used to this sound that it became like background music to their ears.

The big, old homes in the town were surrounded by the flat and gentle rolling countryside. The Reagans lived in two rented houses during their stay in Galesburg. Their favorite one was at 1219 North Kellogg on the corner of Fremont Avenue. This three-story house on the bright red brick street would hold many memories for Dutch. Because Kindergarten wasn't part of elementary school at that time, Dutch stayed home with his mother until first grade. She read every night to both her sons, using her finger to point out each word. Very often, she would read to Dutch during the day.

One day, his father rode his bike home for lunch from O. T. Johnson's department, store, where he worked as manager of the shoe department. The store on Main Street was not far away from their home. This particular day Dutch was sprawled on the floor of the sunny front parlor, looking at the newspaper. Jokingly, Jack asked him to read the paper to him. With his finger under each word, he read the 1916 headline from the

Galesburg Evening Mail, "Five States Feel Force of Powder Blast." This was a munitions explosion in a New Jersey factory. He also read about a bomb going off in San Francisco. Jack was shocked that his son could read at the age of five and a half. Proud and excited, he and Nelle called some neighbors to come to their house to see how their youngest son could read before ever attending school.

Two blocks away Dutch would go to first grade and part of second grade at the Silas Willard School, a big, brick, fortress looking building with its eight classrooms. Here, he received high grades, especially in math and spelling. His classroom was on the front corner, facing Fremont. About fifteen students were in his class. The basement was used for the gym and school plays. In fact, Nelle and Jack would perform occasionally in fund raising productions for the school. As always, Nelle was involved in dramatic readings or morality plays for her church. This was a passion she continued to pursue everywhere they moved.

Dutch's bedroom was the small, front room on the second floor, but he enjoyed poking around the attic of their house. There, he found a glass box collection of butterflies and birds' eggs, belonging to their landlord. On the wooden seat in front of the two bright attic windows, Dutch examined every detail.

In his autobiography, this incident was recalled vividly, "I escaped for hours at a time into the attic, marveling at the rich colors of the eggs and the intricate and fragile wings of the butterflies. The experience left me with a reverence for the handiwork of God that never left me."

There were sad memories of his father from Galesburg. Dark secrets remained in the Reagan home. Sometimes, Jack would disappear for several days. After he returned, Dutch could hear arguments between Nelle and Jack late at night. Nelle would not talk about these secrets until the boys were a little older.

Yet again, his father had to find another job and the Reagans had to leave this delightful town of Galesburg to move 20 miles west to the much smaller town of Monmouth, Illinois, known as the Maple City for its many maple trees. Their white house at 218 South 7th Street was much more modest than the Galesburg one.

Monmouth College was nearby their house. In winter Dutch, Neil, and the Field brothers from next door took their sleds and toboggans over to the college and sledded down the hill. In summer they would hike through the campus or pick grapes from a neighbor's yard. The Field brothers' sister, Kathryn, remembered how well dressed the Reagan boys were in their knickers and shirts. Nelle made most of the clothes for her sons. Dutch skipped the rest of second grade and was put in third grade at the big Central School, which looked very much like a castle with steeples—something out of *Harry Potter*. The giggling girls at Central chased Dutch home when he was a new boy in class and hoped he might show some interest in them. Perhaps, Jack Reagan's drunken experiences in the local tavern caused Dutch too much shame to make friends with these girls.

Jack Reagan worked in the shoe department of E. B. Colwell's on Main Street. The Reagans would have three different rental homes in Monmouth until Jack had a call from his old boss in Tampico, Mr. Pitney. The new owner of his store had died and Mr. Pitney had to take over the business once again. Mr. Pitney asked Jack to come back and run it.

5

A Boyhood of Fun and Sports

Returning to Tampico, Illinois in the summer of 1919 would prove a happy time for the Reagans. Beyond the borders of Illinois, they would read about the first commercial airplane flight between Paris and London. They would learn that United Artists, a Hollywood film company, was formed. Lady Astor, an American from Virginia, would be the first woman elected to the British parliament.

During their second residence in Tampico, the Reagans would live above the H.C. Pitney store. For Dutch, this was an idyllic period. From his upstairs apartment, he could look across to his friend, Harold Monkey Mitchell. They had all sorts of codes and signals to determine their plans. One time the Mitchells invited the Reagans over to visit. Dutch and Monk were playing in Monk's room when Monk decided to get his father's rifle to show Dutch. He pulled the trigger for fun and it exploded, tearing a hole from the ceiling. As the parents rushed into the room, Dutch and Monk grabbed some papers and books to pretend nothing had happened. Terrified, they were reading upside down. Although relieved the boys were unharmed, Jack gave his son a severe tongue-lashing.

These preteen years were happy ones for Dutch. The funeral director and furniture dealer, Mack Parent, didn't have children of his own, so he gathered a group of nine and ten-year-old boys together to play ice hockey on the frozen fields with broomsticks or to play "Fox-and-Goose" (a game of tag) in the snow. He coached the boys in football in the fall and trained them in baseball in the spring. Dutch was better at football. Because his eyesight was so poor, he couldn't see the ball coming at him in baseball. Swimming was the most fun on hot, humid days in summer. Mr. Parent would take the boys a mile out of town to the Hennepin Feeder Canal. In those days, canals were built to accommodate barges that brought supplies to isolated towns and farm communities. Tampico was a safe place to teach boys how to swim. They splashed and swam like tadpoles. Sometimes fish would tickle their toes and small, wild animals would run away from the screams of laughter. Branches of leafy trees hung over the canal. They would swing and jump into the water from them. If a tornado spun above the horizon, they had plenty of time to pack up and get home. At other times, Mack Parent took the boys fishing…just like a real parent.

Dutch and neighbor Chuck Aldredge used to dress up Chuck's cat and his grandfather's dachshund. They would concoct a little tent and give shows, charging safety pins and pennies for admission. Another friend, Stanley Glassburn, and Dutch often went to a farm to ride the old horse "Bird," owned by Stanley's uncle. Afterwards, they would jump in the hay. Dutch's love of horses began at this early age and became a very important part of his life in later years.

The most unpleasant chore Jack Reagan gave his sons was to sort out a truckload of potatoes, throwing out the squishy rotten ones. Dutch never forgot the awful smell from those potatoes and developed a dislike for that vegetable.

These carefree days soon came to an end. Mr. Pitney decided to sell his store and go into business with Jack Reagan in Dixon, Illinois—only 65 miles northeast of Tampico. They planned to establish a Fashion Boot Store. Jack was fascinated by the bone structure of feet and fitting people with proper shoes. The whole Reagan family packed their belongings once again. Nelle was sorry to leave her church and the Opera House, where she and her husband performed, and sad to give up the speech lessons she taught to children and adults. The Reagan sons, too, were sad to move again, but this appeared to be a promising change.

6

A Lifeguard to Remember

The flat land around Dixon, Illinois, fans out in all directions. Trees frame the cornfields and dairy farms. Sunsets in bands of peach and pink seem to stretch along the horizon like endless ribbons. Dixon itself is cut in half by Rock River, called the Hudson of the West. From the River, the town rises like a camel's hump to its famous memorial arch.

Settling into Dixon, Illinois, from 1920 to 1932 gave the Reagans the first real roots they had. In his adult years Ronald Reagan would say, "All of us have a place to go back to; Dixon is that place for me. I think growing up in a small town is a good foundation for anyone who decides to enter politics. You get to know people as individuals, not as blocs or members of special interest groups. You discover that, despite their differences, most people have a lot in common: Every individual is unique, but we all want freedom and liberty, peace, love, and security, a good home, and a chance to worship God in our own way; we all want the chance to get ahead and make our children's lives better than our own. We all want the chance to work at a job of our own choosing and to be fairly rewarded for it and the opportunity to control our own destiny."

Dixon was famous for another president who fought against the Black Hawk Indians in Dixon around 1832 when he was a cadet. That man was Abraham Lincoln.

Many events would be unfolding in America during Dutch's boyhood and teen years. The frivolous Flappers represented an era where women were wild and unconventional. The Flappers skyrocketed to popularity in the 1920s. By October 24, 1929, the stock market took a steep nose-dive and crashed, leaving millions without jobs and food. In 1924, Metro Goldwyn and Mayer film studios merged to become MGM. Charles Lindbergh would make the first airplane flight across the Atlantic Ocean in 1927, followed by Amelia Earhart in 1929. The first Academy Awards began in 1929 just before the economic crash.

Known as the city of pink petunias, Dixon had a population of 10,000. The 200-yard-wide Rock River divides the north and south sides, where young Reagan and his friends ice-skated in winter with their coats flapping like sails. At the top of South Galena Avenue was the white Memorial Arch for World War I with DIXON emblazoned in black letters. Near the river's edge, the cement factory belched a powder of gritty gray dust that deposited its ghostly soot everywhere in town.

Of the five homes the Reagans rented, the two-story, gabled house at 816 South Hennepin Avenue was by far their grandest. As a national historic site, it has been restored as Reagan's boyhood home. There, the Reagan boys and the O'Malley boys across the street played football in the side yard or behind the O'Malleys house. Inside his house, Dutch loosened a tile from the fire hearth to hide a few pennies from his brother in case of an emergency. South Central School, which has been restored as a historic Museum for Ronald Reagan, including his portrait made out of 14,000 jellybeans and a room restored as a replica of his sixth grade classroom, was a few blocks away. The First Christian Church was down at the corner of 2nd Street and Hennepin. Here, Nelle and Dutch would attend three times on Sundays. Nelle also would continue her drama activities and make visits to the local jail to take food to the prisoners. Nelle and Jack continued to teach their sons to be kind to those who were poor and to be tolerant of those of different races and religions.

Those early Dixon years were filled with a boy's recollection of great adventures. Dutch went on camping trips down Rock River with his playmates, pretending to be 19th century explorers. Above the limestone cliffs, he played "Cowboys and Indians" while trying to trap muskrats along the river. Feeding the squirrels was a lifelong passion that he continued at the White House in walking to the Oval Office each day. Dutch loved a small town where everyone knew everyone else. In time of need, Dixon people were there to help. If someone's barn burned down, neighbors would help rebuild it.

At times, Dutch was a mischief-maker like his brother. Illegal fireworks were banned in Dixon on the fourth of July, but somehow Dutch managed to get hold of a blockbuster firework, called a torpedo. He set it off on the town bridge. As he was congratulating himself, a police car pulled alongside him, and an officer insisted he get in. Once in the car, Dutch made a smart aleck remark to the policeman that landed him a fine of $14.50. Jack Reagan was called to come down to the station to pay the fine. It took a long time before Dutch could pay his father what he owed.

Unfortunately, Jack Reagan had a weakness for alcohol. Nelle tried to make her sons be patient and not condemn their father. She called it a sickness—a disease. One incident was seared in Dutch's memory. "When I was eleven, I came home from the YMCA one cold, blustery winter's night. My mother was gone on one of her sewing jobs and I expected the house to be empty. As I walked up the stairs, I nearly stumbled over a lump near the front door; it was Jack lying in the snow, his arms outstretched and flat on his back. I leaned over to see what was wrong and smelled whiskey. He had found his way home from a speakeasy (a place where alcohol was sold illegally) and had just passed out right there. For a moment or two, I looked down at him and thought about continuing on into the house and going to bed as if he weren't there. But I couldn't do it. When I tried to wake him he just snored—loud enough, I suspected, for the whole neighborhood to hear him. So I grabbed a piece of his overcoat, pulled it, and dragged him into the house, then put him to bed and never mentioned the incident to my mother."

When Jack Reagan was sober, he was a compassionate as well as a funny man. It also was said that sometimes he would not have a drink for two years. One day, he was standing outside his shoe store in Dixon as a friend passed by with his son. Jack asked how everything was going and his friend said that he didn't have enough money to buy shoes for his son. Jack insisted the boy come inside. He measured his foot and gave the boy a free pair of shoes.

The frequent moves of the Reagan family made Dutch very cautious in making friends. "Although I always had lots of play-mates, during those first years in Dixon I was a little introverted and probably a little slow in making really close friends. In some ways, I think this reluctance to get close to people never left me completely. I've never had trouble making friends, but I've been inclined to hold back a little of myself, reserving it for myself," he recalled in his autobiography.

Although Dutch worked on the yearbook drawing cartoons and other little sketches, his own name was misspelled in the 1928 *Dixonian*. The name Donald Reagan appeared alongside his photograph. Maybe he didn't mind because his parents had considered naming him Donald before they settled on Ronald. Underneath his picture, he wrote, "Life is just one grand, sweet song, so start the music."

From 1926 to 1932 Dutch became a summer lifeguard at the 300-acre Lowell Park, named after the poet James Russell Lowell whose family gave the land to the town, on Rock River to earn money for college at $15 a week until he reached $20 a week. On his way down to the River, Ronald Reagan had a special spot that looked down on the bend in the river above the treetops. He would stop there to scan the view. Every time, his heart filled with joy and he couldn't wait to reach the water's edge.

Mrs. Graybill, the manager's wife, let Dutch eat as many hamburgers and drink as much root beer as he wanted because she thought he was much too thin. Hamburgers were sold from the bathhouse (now restored) for ten cents and root beer for five cents.

The lifeguard chair was set in the water, so he could watch all the swimmers. The current was deceptive and could drag a swimmer down in seconds. Those swimming lessons in Tampico were invaluable. Dutch rescued a total of 77 people from the swift current in the river. Every time he saved someone, he made a notch with a small ax on a big log, which eventually was lost in a flood. It was rumored that many young girls swooned over this good-looking young man and pretended to drown, hoping he would save them. Reagan's response to that rumor was, "I'd never get my suit wet if there was no need for it." However, he was flattered by this speculation.

Dutch had business sense as well. He would rent the canoes to young lovers, who wanted to paddle the boats on the river and serenade their girl friends. When he went out himself, he would bring a hand-cranked Victrola to play records. One of his favorites was "Ramona," which he played over and over. One friend became so sick of the song that he threw the record overboard.

Trying to get to his assigned place as lifeguard was not always easy. If Dutch couldn't get a ride on the Graybill truck, he would hitchhike to the entrance of Lowell Park and then cut through the steep trails until he reached the bottom where he could climb up to his chair in Rock River, ready to rescue anyone in need. The River is almost 200 miles long, starting in Wisconsin, going south, slightly north, and south again until reaching the Mississippi River at Davenport, Iowa, or the Quad Cities.

From the influence of his mother, Dutch began his quest for reading books. He read all the *Rover Boys* series and Mark Twain. His mother gave him *Northern Lights* because of his interest in nature. *That Printer of Udell's* by Harold Wright, *Tarzan* and *Frank Merriwell at Yale* were among his favorites. Books about college life inspired him to strive for this unreachable dream—going to college. Dutch also memorized the ballads, "The Shooting of Dan McGrew" and the "Cremation of Sam McGee." Nelle had always told her sons, "You will never be alone if you read a book."

In Dixon, Nelle tried again to interest her sons in participating in dramatic readings. Neil began to perform and was an instant success with audiences, but Dutch remained reluctant and shy. Finally, Dutch consented because of sibling rivalry with his brother. "Summoning up my courage, I walked up to the stage that night, cleared my throat, and made my theatrical debut. I don't remember what I said, but I'll never forget the response: People laughed and applauded...when I walked off the stage that night, my life had changed."

Another change was about to alter his life. At the age of thirteen or fourteen, the Reagan family had gone for a Sunday drive. Neil and Dutch sat in the back. Nelle had left her glasses on the backseat and Dutch put them on for a joke. His blurred eyesight was changed in an instant. "By picking up my mother's glasses, I had discovered that I was extremely nearsighted. A new world suddenly opened up to me. The reason I'd been such a lousy baseball player was that I couldn't see a pitch until it was about three feet from me. Now I knew why I'd always been the last kid chosen for the baseball team. And I also knew why I'd always jockeyed to get a desk in the front row at school. I hadn't realized that the other kids could see the blackboard from the back of the room. The next day I was fitted for glasses."

Those glasses were horn-rimmed and Dutch was teased because of them, but he didn't care since he could see. He kept the glasses with him in his Lifeguard chair, but never wore them when he rescued people. Many years later, when contact lenses were perfected, Reagan would wear only one lens. Somehow, his other eye would readjust and he was able to see near and far. Vanity was also part of the reason for shifting to contact lenses, especially in the acting profession.

Next, Dutch couldn't wait to get to high school.

7

High School Football and Young Love

Once Dutch reached high school, he felt that he was all grown up. So much so, that he and Neil decided to ask their parents if they could call them Nelle and Jack rather than Mother and Dad. Surprised by the request, Nelle and Jack agreed that their sons made a reasonable request. Neil, too, gained a nickname from his friends. He had a best friend, Winston McReynolds. Wherever Neil was, Winston was there and vice versa. The favorite comic strip of that era was "Moon Mullins." The two characters were "Moon" and "Mushmouth." Neil became known as "Moon" and Winston as "Mushmouth." No one ever called his brother "Neil" again, except Nelle. It was Moon for the rest of his life. Dutch was still Dutch to everyone, except Nelle.

Because Dutch loved the game of football more than any other sport, he couldn't wait to get on the team. The only problem was that Dutch weighed 108 pounds and was only five feet three inches tall as a freshman of thirteen-years-old because he had skipped second grade. When the coach looked at him, he didn't have the heart to kick him off the team. However, there weren't any uniforms to fit this pip-squeak player. Finally, the coach found some shoulder pads and a helmet, but finding football pants was virtually impossible. Somewhere he dug up an antique pair with bamboo thigh pads. It didn't matter, Dutch was happy.

Fortunately, there were two high schools in Dixon: one on the North side and one on the South side. The Reagans had lived on both sides of the Rock River. Neil was attending South Dixon High School when the family moved to the North side. Neil decided to stay at South Dixon High since his football career was well launched there and he was a football hero. This was a welcome decision for Dutch. When he entered North Dixon High School, which is now a nursing home, he didn't have to compete against his brother, but his small stature was a handicap.

Dutch sat on the football bench all of his freshman year. His body frame was not growing. He decided to take a summer job working for a construction company to build his muscles. He swung a pick shovel and learned how to shingle, lay floors, and pour concrete at thirty-five cents an hour. In the future, he used these skills on his ranches.

Sophomore year was a little more promising. The school created a second football team for those under 135 pounds. His teammates elected Dutch to be their captain. Now, Ronald Reagan would be part of the action. He loved the tangle of bodies during his turns as tackle and guard. Breaking through the opposition's line was a thrill for him and he loved wearing the purple and white jersey.

Besides his love of football, Dutch found something else to engage his heart and mind in his sophomore year—romance. A new minister had come to his mother's church and his daughter, Margaret Cleaver, captivated Dutch Reagan's heart. They say that children look for someone like their parent as a possible mate. Apparently, Margaret or "Mugs," as she was affectionately nicknamed, looked very much like Nelle—petite and pretty. Dutch was sure that Margaret would become his wife in the future. But Margaret was upset by Jack Reagan's drinking and it almost ended their romance. Dutch tried to explain his father's problem as a disease. Eventually, Margaret came to accept Jack's occasional binges, and their romance continued.

Among Dutch's many activities was that of a drum major for the YMCA band. One time when he was leading the band and twirling his baton, he kept marching straight ahead while the rest of the band turned left. Many observers have interpreted this incident as symbolic of Reagan's political life as a man who marched to his own drumbeat.

Another of Dutch's teenage discoveries came through his English teacher, B. J. Frazer, a rather small bespectacled man, who had a great love of theatre. Frazer told his English class that their essays would be judged on originality. Dutch submitted many original essays, which Frazer found delightful. He began asking Dutch to read them in front of the class. When his classmates laughed at his stories, it felt good to him. Dutch started trying out for high school productions that Frazer directed. He liked Frazer's method of directing, giving the actor an opportunity to explore the feelings of his character.

About those early theatrical experiences, Ronald Reagan said, "As I've grown older, perhaps there's always been a little of that small boy inside me who found some reassurance in the applause and approval he first heard at nine or ten. But in high school, I began to lose my feelings of insecurity: success in the school plays, in football and swimming, being the only guy on the beach with LIFE GUARD on my chest, and saving seventy-seven people, being elected student body president, even the fact I could now see, did a lot to give me self-confidence. Still, I think there's something about the entertainment world that attracts people who may have had youthful feelings of shyness or insecurity."

Meanwhile, Dutch was growing tall and broad during his junior and senior years. He became student body president as well as something of a sports hero. He finally got off the football bench when a teammate couldn't play right guard. The coach sent him to play that position. Dutch played so well that he stayed on the first team for the next two years and became a football hero for Dixon's North High School. At last, he fulfilled his teenage dream.

8

A Poor Boy's Dream of College

After graduating from high school, Dutch thought that it would be almost impossible for him to go to college. He had saved $400 from his many jobs, including his summers as a lifeguard, but that was not enough for tuition and room and board. He found that working in his father's shoe store was far from his liking. His father made it very clear that he was not able to contribute anything to his college education. His brother didn't see the need for college and instead, he had gone from high school into Dixon's cement factory and made more money than his father. But Dutch still held to his dream of going to college.

Two factors kept this dream alive. A minister's son, who had been a football hero in Dixon as a quarterback, had gone to the church's Eureka College about two hours away from Dixon. There, he had excelled on the football team as a quarterback. Secondly, Dutch's girl friend, Margaret Cleaver, had decided to go to Eureka just like two of her sisters. To follow his girl friend was another driving factor.

When the day came for Margaret to leave for Eureka, Dutch went with the Cleavers to take their daughter to college. It was almost 120 miles southeast of Dixon. They drove through the scenic, pristine land, inhabited by Scandinavians, whose farmhouses were carefully groomed and farm machinery was freshly painted. Soon, the Cleavers approached the factory town of Peoria, Illinois. From Peoria were long stretches of flat prairies until twenty miles east was the turn off to the hilly town of Eureka with a population of 2,000 at that time. It was also known as the pumpkin capital of Illinois.

As soon as Dutch saw the Christian College of Eureka, he was impressed. It was set on a hill on 112 acres, far away from the world. Like umbrellas, the elm and maple trees towered above the five Georgian brick buildings, positioned over the sloping quadrangle where 250 students would go from class to class.

Immediately smitten, Dutch was determined to find a way to be part of Eureka and stay. While Margaret was registering, Dutch found coach Ralph (Mac) McKinzie to persuade him to provide a football scholarship to cover the $180 tuition. He did. He found special money in a Needy Student Scholarship to cover at least half of the tuition. To cover the cost of an attic room and meals, Dutch washed dishes at the Teke (Tau Kappa Epsilon) fraternity house where he was accepted as a pledge. This scholarship would be good for one year.

Margaret and Dutch remained a steady couple. In fact, Dutch gave her his TKE fraternity pin to wear, which was almost a gesture of a pre-engagement. Both were busy, but they managed to sip and share twenty cent cherry phosphates at the local drugstore in the charming town of Eureka. Or they would spend romantic moments in a local cemetery where other young lovers met. The couples would sit on blankets and lean up against tombstones to exchange the secrets of their souls in between kisses and holding hands.

As a freshman, Dutch was thrust into the center of campus politics. The upperclassmen appointed him to give a speech at midnight in the chapel to call for college president Bert Wilson's resignation. Because of the failing economy in 1929, Wilson wanted to cut courses and reduce the faculty. This meant that seniors wouldn't be able to graduate without these courses. If the students went home for Thanksgiving, they were afraid that the cuts would take place in their absence. Therefore, all the students decided to stay and protest. When the Thanksgiving weekend was over, the students went on strike by not attending classes, but Dutch Reagan's speech on that Saturday night forced the resignation.

"Because I was a freshman and didn't have the same vested interests in avoiding the faculty cutbacks that upperclassmen did, I was chosen to present our committee's proposal for a strike. I reviewed how the cutbacks threatened not only the diplomas of upperclassmen, but also the academic reputation of Eureka; I described how the administration had ignored us when we tried to present alternate ideas for saving money and then planned to pull off the coup in secrecy while we were gone from college. Giving that speech—my first—was as exciting as any I ever gave. For the first time in my life, I felt my words reach out and grab an audience, and it was exhilarating. When I'd say something, they'd roar after every sentence, sometimes every word, and after a while, it was as if the audience and I were one." Reagan always remembered this episode as his first experience in college politics.

After the president resigned, Dutch returned to his studies in economics and sociology while participating in theatrical productions, directed by acting teacher, Miss Ellen Johnson. Dutch also took elocution lessons from Elizabeth McKinzie, the coach's wife.

However, that first year at Eureka was disappointing for Dutch. He sat on the football bench without playing a single game. He was sure the coach didn't like him. When he went back to Dixon for the summer to lifeguard at Lowell Park, he wondered whether Eureka was the right place for him. Through a high school friend, he met someone who was sure he could get Dutch a scholarship on the crew team at the University of Wisconsin. Without any funds to return to Eureka, this seemed the best solution.

However, once again, he joined the Cleaver family in their journey to Margaret's second year at Eureka. Dutch was sad at the prospect of not being near Margaret. Everyone was glad to see Dutch, but disappointed that he wasn't returning to college. Even coach McKinzie seemed sad, but Dutch told him that he didn't have any money. Once again, the coach dipped into the Needy Student Scholarship fund. He offered the same deal to Dutch, except the TKE house couldn't offer him the dishwashing job. To cover room and board, Mac arranged for Dutch to wash dishes at the girl's dormitory, Lyda Wood—an enviable position for a handsome young man. Becoming a swimming coach also would be part of his scholarship duties. Dutch called his mother to ask her to send his clothes to college.

In another twist of fate, Neil Reagan decided that shoveling limestone for three years at the cement factory was taking him nowhere. He wanted to go to college. Dutch managed to persuade the coach to take Neil on scholarship as a freshman football player. Neil pledged the same fraternity and waited tables, serving his younger brother as a sophomore. And so, the sibling rivalry continued.

By his sophomore year, Dutch was still sitting on the football bench. Neil had no trouble getting on the team. Dutch had to impress Mac McKinzie. During a block and tackle practice, Dutch hit the assistant coach so hard that he flew up in the air. McKinzie was impressed and sent Dutch on the field for two minutes of game time during every game.

When the team traveled away from Eureka to play, there was always a question as to whether the hotels would accept their black players. One time they went to Dixon and spent the night in the Dixon hotel. The coach wanted Dutch to stay there, too. But the hotel manager refused to accommodate the two "coloreds." The coach was prepared to have the team spend the night in the bus. Dutch had a better solution. He offered to take the two boys home with him and say that there wasn't enough room in the hotel for everyone. Nelle opened her door and her heart to Dutch and his two teammates. "She was absolutely colorblind when it came to racial matters; those fellows were just two of my friends. That was the way she and Jack had always raised my brother and me," Reagan observed in his autobiography.

Not unlike other young men of that age, Ronald Reagan experimented with alcohol at college. "It was during Prohibition and a lot of movies depicted illicit drinking as 'collegiate' and I guess I was curious about the effects of alcohol. One night Moon and I were visiting two fraternity brothers who worked for a doctor and in return received the free use of his apartment; they had a bottle and started passing it around. Even with all the experience I'd had with Jack's drinking, I didn't know anything about the effect of highballs; so when the bottle came to me, I'd take a big drink, as if it was a bottle of soda pop. Well, they soon decided I was so blind drunk that they couldn't take me back to the fraternity house in my condition. Inside, I thought I was sober. I'd try to say something intelligent but what came out of my mouth would make Moon and my fraternity brothers fall down laughing. They took me out of town and walked me along a country road, one on each side, trying to make me sober. But it didn't do a lot of good, so they brought me back to the fraternity house and threw me in a shower…I woke up the next day with a terrible hangover. That was it for me. I decided if that's what you get for drinking—a sense of helplessness—I didn't want any part of it."

By 1930 the famous economic Depression hit the country very hard. Nelle and Jack were victims, too. Jack's Fashion Boot Shop went out of business because people just didn't have the money to buy high quality shoes. Nelle went to work at a dress shop as a seamstress clerk and earned $14 a week while Jack went on the road looking for work. Nelle finally had to ask her youngest son if she could borrow fifty dollars from him, swearing him to secrecy—a secret kept from Jack. Without hesitation he gave it to her. Jack finally found a job as a shoe clerk in Springfield, Illinois, which was 200 miles from Dixon. When Moon and Dutch were playing a football game in Springfield, they persuaded Mac to let them visit their father. The sight of his father living in a poor neighborhood and working in a garish shoe store brought tears to Dutch's eyes. Silently, Dutch prayed for his father. "I have always prayed a lot; in those days I prayed things would get better for our country, for our family, and for Dixon. I even prayed before football games. I prayed no one would be injured, we'd all do our best and have no regrets no matter how the game came out."

During his four years at Eureka, Dutch had acted in fourteen theatrical productions. In his senior year, Dutch's acting instructor, Ellen Johnson, prepared a one-act play to take to a contest at Northwestern University outside Chicago. It was *Aria da Capo,* written by American poet Edna St. Vincent Millay. Dutch was cast in the part of a shepherd who is strangled at the very end. He loved playing this death scene. Eureka placed second, competing against many prestigious colleges. Afterwards, the head of Northwestern's speech department approached Dutch and indicated that the young actor might have a future in the profession. Dutch was surprised and flattered, but his secret hopes were in radio. He wanted to become a sports announcer. Often at the fraternity house, he would grab a broom, pretending to be a sportscaster, replaying the latest football or baseball games locally or nationally. His fraternity brothers were amused as much as they were entertained.

As graduation approached, it became evident that Dutch and Margaret would not be going back to Dixon together. Her father had become the minister in Eureka. Also, Margaret had found a teaching position at a high school in a small town in rural Illinois. Dutch would be returning to his lifeguard job in Dixon for the last summer. He had college debts to pay and it gave him time to think through his future plans. Finding a job in 1932 wasn't easy. But Margaret and Dutch still wrote letters to each other because they had become engaged during their senior year. After Dutch graduated, he met a businessman in Dixon who offered to help him. The man didn't have any contacts in radio, although he suggested Dutch get a job in a small station and work as hard as he could for the next step.

However, Dutch wanted to try breaking into the Chicago world of radio. He hitchhiked to the Windy City, trying to find a job without success. The people in the radio stations all laughed at him because he had no experience in being a radio announcer. A secretary took pity on him and told him to go to a radio station somewhere out in a country area to get experience. Disappointed, Dutch returned home to Dixon. Jack Reagan was sympathetic to his son's ambitions and loaned him the family car, an Oldsmobile. Dutch drove southwest to work his way up the Mississippi River on the Illinois side, stopping at small radio stations. None of them needed him. By then, he was almost at Davenport, Iowa, where Rock River spills into the Mississippi River.

Would he ever find a job?

9

Iowa Hires a Sportscaster

Shortly after Dutch graduated from Eureka College in 1932, Franklin Delano Roosevelt was elected president of the United States. All the Reagans were Democrats and supported F.D.R. In Europe, Adolf Hitler became President of Germany in 1934. Between 1934 and 1935, Mao Tse Tung of China marched 6,000 miles to spread his philosophy of communism. By 1935 President Roosevelt started Social Security for the jobless and elderly.

Dutch Reagan's world was to find a job. He headed to Iowa, seeking his first of many dreams. Iowa was different from Illinois. The land was rolling and much more rugged. The fields were not as straight and flat. The bluish gray sky framed the autumn colors of rust, gold, and mauve along the Rock River, which flows along the Mississippi River until they come together. The bridge across the Mississippi into Davenport made a dramatic entrance for the college graduate.

When Dutch crossed the border of Illinois in his hunt for a job, he stopped at WOC in Davenport. It was located on the rooftop of the School of Chiropractic building at Palmer College, overlooking the river. Dutch was awed by the blue velvet drapes, which were to absorb the sounds, in the radio studio of WOC (World of Chiropractic). He impressed a crusty Scots program director, Peter MacArthur, with a vivid description of a fourth quarter football game at Eureka College against Western University. The expressionless Scotsman hired him at five dollars plus bus fare to cover the Iowa/Minnesota football game. Dutch had his foot in the door of the radio business. He researched information about the players on both teams. Listening to Dutch's coverage of the game in Iowa City, MacArthur was impressed once again by his performance. He offered Dutch a job to cover ten games of the season at ten dollars a game plus bus fare. In one week, he had doubled his salary.

Once the football season was over, MacArthur didn't have an opening for him. Dutch went back to Dixon, wondering what to do next. Following New Year's Day, MacArthur called Dutch to say a staff announcer had left and did he want a job as a regular radio announcer at $100 a month? Today, a sportscaster might get $5,000 a month. Dutch was thrilled. He returned immediately to Davenport and started as a disc jockey. Reading the commercials in a conversational way was difficult for him, so some of his colleagues coached him on how to do it.

One night he was playing organ music sponsored by the local mortuary and decided not to read the commercial. Dutch was unaware of the financial importance between advertisers and programming. The next day the advertiser was so angry that MacArthur was forced to fire Dutch. They wanted him to stay long enough to train his replacement, who was moving from a teacher's job to announcer. When the trainee heard how Dutch was fired, he decided not to leave the teaching profession. Dutch's job was saved temporarily.

Meanwhile, the Reagan family in Dixon was on a financial roller coaster. Jack Reagan was able to become manager of a division of the WPA, Works Progress Administration, created by Franklin D. Roosevelt during the Depression. Jack helped people find jobs and he even handed out foodstuffs. Although Jack was an excellent administrator, he had to give up working altogether because of heart trouble. Dutch began sending part of his monthly salary home to his parents and sent Moon ten dollars a month to pay for some of his expenses in college.

The offices of WOC closed within three months and many of the staff members were transferred to WHO, the sister station in Des Moines, Iowa. They specifically hired Dutch to be a sports announcer for football, baseball, and track at $100 a month. Soon, Dutch would be making seventy-five dollars a week. The initials WHO stood for With Hands Open, meaning to help each other.

Des Moines was a thriving city. The beautiful gold dome of the state house could be seen from anywhere in the city. Dutch loved working at WHO and found an apartment at 400 Center Street. The WHO radio listeners stretched from Mexico to New Zealand. Dutch couldn't have been happier.

However, one part of his life turned from happiness to sorrow. A letter arrived from Margaret Cleaver. When he opened it, his TKE pin and the engagement ring that he had given her during their senior year in college fell out. The letter told him of how she had met a U.S. foreign-service officer on a ship going to Europe and had fallen in love with him. She planned to be married in a matter of weeks. Dutch was devastated. In a telephone conversation with his mother, Nelle said that perhaps for some reason this was part of God's plan. Eventually, Dutch's broken heart recovered.

During Dutch's four years in Des Moines, he met and dated many young ladies. The women in the radio station were particularly struck by his good looks. He even had an occasion to play the part of a rescuer in real life. When a nurse from out of town stepped off the bus late one night, she began walking to the hospital to assume her duties, but was confronted by a robber. In his upstairs apartment, Dutch heard the scuffle. He leaned out his window with an unloaded 45 automatic gun and shouted, "Leave her alone or I'll shoot you between the shoulders!" The robber dropped the woman's purse and suitcase and ran. Dutch came downstairs in his pajamas and bathrobe to see if the woman was all right. He then walked her to the hospital to be sure that she was safe. The role of lifeguard never seemed to leave him.

There were funny times at the WHO radio station, too, because Dutch was a practical joker. Most of the time Dutch attended the Chicago Cubs' baseball games, in person, but when he didn't, the radio operator would receive the plays over the telegraph by Morse code and then slide the information to Dutch through a glass window between the control room and his studio. Dutch could ad-lib and deliver exciting descriptions of each play. Suddenly, the wire went dead and he didn't know what the next play was. He stalled and stalled by saying the player kept hitting pop ups or foul balls. Then, he would describe the weather over Wrigley Field in Chicago. This went on for seven minutes, but somehow Dutch recovered and people stopped him on the street, asking him about all those pop ups and foul balls. He never admitted to anything.

After Moon Reagan graduated from Eureka, he came to visit Dutch in Des Moines. During one of Dutch's programs, Moon was invited to come sit inside the studio. As Dutch began his predictions about future games, Moon shook his head in disagreement. Dutch told the listening audience about his brother and asked Moon to come over to the microphone, so they could discuss and disagree on the air. It was so popular that the station hired Moon. Long term, Moon became program director for the station before joining an advertising agency in Los Angeles and becoming its vice-president.

Jim Zabel took over Dutch's job as sports announcer after Dutch finally left the station, but recalled him as a "charming man and sharp as a tack." He said that Ronald Reagan's voice had "good inflection, color, and movement." Over the years, Zabel interviewed Reagan eighteen times.

After the disappointment over Margaret, Dutch turned to a new interest in riding horses. At Fort Des Moines, twenty miles south of Des Moines, Dutch took classes with the 14th Cavalry Regiment to inspire his new passion. Amid the long red stables and dense woods, Dutch rode horseback. He especially liked riding a horse by the name of Red Ace. On May 25, 1937, Ronald Reagan received the commission of second lieutenant in the Officers' Reserve Corps of the Cavalry. During the day of his long test on his horse, the rain soaked the rider and made the ground soggy. On the final unexpected jump, Dutch hung onto the horse's mane as they soared above a stack of telephone poles to land safely in the muddy track beyond. Dutch passed the course and knew that some time in the future he wanted to own a ranch and have horses.

However, life was about to take Ronald Reagan in a new direction beyond the microphones of radio.

10

A Hollywood Screen Test

Iowa winters were long, dreary, and bitterly cold. Dutch devised a scheme where he could avoid part of it. To his manager, he suggested covering the Chicago Cubs' spring training for two weeks on Catalina Island off the coast of California—all expenses paid. After WHO agreed to his idea, starting in 1935, Dutch hopped on a train and headed for California. Every year the dreams of sunny California were exactly what he lived for. He wrote articles for the Des Moines newspapers to fatten the extra costs of his trip as well as broadcasting for WHO.

By 1937 Ronald Reagan was addicted to the warmth and color of California. On this trip to cover spring training, he decided to hop on a boat to the mainland and go see a famous Iowa band called *The Oklahoma Outlaws*. They were being filmed in a Gene Autry movie at Republic Studios. Dutch located the Studios and watched his friends in the group play on the movie set. He found all the cameras, lights, and sound effects dazzling. Memories of theatrical productions at Eureka College stirred anew.

After the filming, he tried to go back to Catalina, but a storm and floods prevented him. He booked himself into the Biltmore Hotel in Los Angeles where the Cubs often stayed during exhibition games. He noticed that the Biltmore Bowl nightclub was featuring a girl from Iowa, Joy Hodges, who used to come to the WHO studios and sing. She had left Des Moines to become a successful singer and starlet in movies. He decided to look her up and sent a note backstage to see if she would join him for dinner between her two evening shows. She accepted. He liked Joy because she was so unaffected by Hollywood. Over dinner, he confided in her that he had always had a desire to be an actor. Reluctantly, he asked her if she thought that he could be a movie actor.

"Stand up," she said. "Take off those black-rimmed glasses and never put them on again." She thought the young man had possibilities. He had a good-looking face and was a gorgeous hunk of a man.

Joy Hodges set up an appointment with her agents, Bill Meiklejohn and George Ward. Meiklejohn called Max Arnow, a casting agent, and said, "I have the next Robert Taylor sitting in my office." Arnow was not impressed, but he told Meiklejohn to send him over. Dutch removed his glasses at the interview and tried to project star quality—whatever that was. Arnow was more intrigued by Dutch's voice than his looks. They arranged a screen test for Dutch at Warner Brothers the next day. Dutch hurriedly caught the last boat to Catalina to return to his broadcasting duties. The manager was very mad at Dutch because of his absence. It wasn't like him. The next day Dutch took another boat to the mainland and went to Warner Brothers Studios, which was like a city within a city, to do a three-minute scene from Philip Barry's *Holiday*.

Once the test was over, Dutch knew he had to return to Iowa and fulfill his duties for broadcasting. Unaware of this, the casting director told Dutch to go back to the hotel and wait a few days for them to process the screen test before they could let him know the outcome and their decision. Dutch informed his agent and casting director how impossible that would be. He had to catch the next train for Iowa to broadcast the Cubs' games. The Hollywood power brokers were stunned. No one had ever refused them. Usually actors were begging to be accepted into show business. Not Dutch. He had promises to keep and a commitment to fulfill.

Shortly after his return to Des Moines, a telegram came from his agent. It read, "Warners offers contract seven years stop one year option stop starting $200 a week stop what shall I do?" Now it was Dutch's turn to be stunned, but thrilled. He sent a telegram right back to Bill Meiklejohn, "Sign before they change their minds."

Within a month, Dutch Reagan had resigned from the WHO radio station, packed his belongings, bought a 1934 Nash Lafayette coupe, and drove to Hollywood to check into the Biltmore Hotel. His agent warned that he might have to wait a long time before any role might come his way. In fact, it took only a few days for the call to come. He was offered the lead role in a B movie, called *Love is on the Air*. He was to play the part of a radio announcer.

Once the film was cast, Dutch was sent to make-up to order his clothes and look at his hairdo. They grumbled over his hair, parted in the middle. They groaned over the fact that his head seemed too small for his broad shoulders and height. What could they do to correct these cosmetic flaws. The hairstyle was no problem. They could fix that. But what could they do about the rest? Then they remembered that actor James Cagney had the same problem—his neck was too short. They contacted

Cagney's shirt-maker, who flattened the collar and instructed Dutch to wear wide ties with big knots. That did the trick. Dutch continued to wear these self-styled shirts in real life because they enhanced his appearance. Because he had such a natural, rosy complexion, Dutch never had to wear makeup.

Next, the publicity department wanted to change his name. Dutch Reagan was not their idea of a matinee idol's name. They tossed around many possible names. Dutch finally said, "What about Ronald Reagan?" They thought that was a great name. So, Ronald Reagan's first name, which he detested as a youth, became a perfect name for a Hollywood actor.

Once *Love is on the Air* reached movie theatres, *Hollywood Reporter* gave the young actor a good review. "*Love is on the Air* presents a new leading man, Ronald Reagan, who is a natural, giving one of the best first picture performances Hollywood has offered in many a day." After that review, Dutch was hired for another movie, *Sergeant Murphy.*

With two successful movies under his belt, Warner Brothers gave him a raise. Reagan called his parents in Dixon and asked them to join him in California. He offered to buy them their first home and enjoy the warmth of California. They accepted and moved as fast as they could.

Ronald Reagan's movie career caught fire. He made thirteen films in the first year and a half. Probably his most famous role was that of George Gipp in *Knute Rockne—All American.* Knute Rockne was a famous coach from Notre Dame that changed the game of football. Rockne was killed in an air crash in 1931. Gipp was one of Rockne's star football players who died. Throughout his film and political career, Reagan referred to a memorable speech George Gipp made on his deathbed, "Some day when things are tough and the breaks are going against the boys, ask them to go in there and win one for the Gipper. I don't know where I'll be but I'll know about it and I'll be happy."

Before the movie was made, Reagan had decided to write a screenplay about Knute Rockne, starring Pat O'Brien. He talked so much about it that one day he heard that the studio was going to make a movie about the coach. They had stolen Reagan's idea. He rushed down to the casting office and told them he wanted to be considered for the part of George Gipp. They dismissed Reagan for the part and said he didn't have the build of a football player. Reagan went home and dug out his Eureka yearbook with pictures of him in his football uniform. Back to the casting office, he tossed the photos on the desk, saying some of the lines as George Gipp. He also told them that George Gipp weighed five pounds less than he did. They were convinced and Ronald Reagan was hired for the part.

Moviegoers were moved to tears by Ronald Reagan's dying scene as George Gipp, and he is remembered decades later for that role. The film was premiered at Notre Dame University in 1940. Ronald Reagan took his father there for the occasion, but was apprehensive about his father's drinking. Jack Reagan remained fairly sober for the event, and it was an unbelievable experience for him. Understandably, Ronald Reagan's parents were proud of their son's success and notoriety.

In a western movie around 1939 and 1940, Reagan lost most of his hearing in his right ear when an actor fired a shot right at his head. He never recovered from that accident, but finally started using a hearing aid in 1983.

Would he ever have time for romance in his life?

11

A New Family and War

The California lifestyle agreed with all the Reagans. Nelle and Jack Reagan had fallen in love with sunny California. Once she and Jack were settled in their new home, Nelle joined a church and became involved in her good works of visiting hospitals, prisoners, and making dinners for the homeless. She also visited the movie sets and became like a mother to all the young actors. Until his death, Jack helped Dutch take care of his fan mail, giving him something to do in their new Hollywood surroundings.

Ronald Reagan's movie career kept him busy. By 1938 he was cast in his ninth film "Brother Rat," a movie about a Virginia Military Institute cadet. A young, pretty actress named Jane Wyman, played opposite Reagan. Although Jane had a previous brief marriage, she became attracted to the good-looking actor. Off the set, romance was growing between the handsome pair. Louella Parsons, a famous Hollywood gossip columnist, was from Dixon, Illinois, and took a special interest in Ronald Reagan. In 1939, she took Reagan and Wyman on a nine-week vaudeville tour around the country, introducing "Stars of Tomorrow" to the American public. Naturally, they made a publicity stop in Dixon. There was a parade and much fanfare for the young man from Dixon and the famous Louella Parsons.

When they flew into Chicago for an appearance, there was a terrible snowstorm. The plane ride was so terrifying that Reagan vowed that he would never fly again. He kept that promise until the 1960s when Ronald Reagan agreed to fly for political appearances.

Not long afterwards, Louella Parsons announced Reagan's engagement to Jane Wyman in her column. They were married in January of 1940 and Louella Parsons gave the reception party. The star-studded couple delighted photographers of movie magazines, placing them on their covers and a spread of pictures inside. Their daughter Maureen Elizabeth was born in January of 1941. Jane and Ronnie doted on the newest member of their family. When their daughter became four-years-old, she took the money out of her piggy bank and went to a toy store in Beverly Hills with her father and asked the shop attendant if she could buy a baby brother, spilling all her pennies on the counter. Surprised by this request, Jane and Ronnie quickly researched the possibility of adoption. Within three weeks, they adopted their son, Michael, in 1945.

The idyllic life of two movie stars and their two children would change after the Japanese air force attacked Pearl Harbor on December 7, 1941. Like many male actors, Reagan tried to enlist in the army. Because his eyesight prevented him from combat, he was assigned to making propaganda and training films in Culver City at the Hal Roach Studios, nicknamed Ft. Roach. There, Reagan became an adjutant and personnel officer. The training films, narrated by Reagan, were sent wherever the army air corps bases were located.

During his time at Ft. Roach, Reagan became disillusioned by the way government operated. At first, the government rejected his request for civilian workers to help with secretarial duties. Suddenly fifty civilian bureaucrats were assigned. "I discovered it was almost impossible to remove an incompetent or lazy worker and that one of the most popular methods supervisors used in dealing with an incompetent was to transfer him or her out of his department to a higher-paying job in another department," Reagan said in his autobiography.

In 1942 Ronald Reagan's other memorable film, *Kings Row*, was released. He had made it before being called to the intelligence unit at Roach Studios. His character, Hugh McDrake, had both legs amputated by a surgeon who despised McDrake for romancing his daughter. When McDrake awakens from the surgery, he discovers his legs missing and cries out, "Where's the rest of me?" This was the title of Reagan's early autobiography and caused him to do some soul-searching.

In his autobiography *Where's the Rest of Me?* Reagan commented, "So much of our profession is taken up with pretending that an actor must spend at least half of his waking hours in fantasy, in rehearsal or shooting. If he is only an actor, I feel, he is much like I was in *Kings Row*, only half a man—no matter how great his talents. I regard acting with the greatest affection; it has made my life for me. But I realize it tends to become an island of exaggerated importance. I began to feel like a shut-in invalid, nursed by publicity. I have always liked space, the feeling of freedom, a broad range of friends, and variety...I loved three things: drama, politics, and sports. In all three of them I came out of the monastery of movies into the world. In politics, I found myself misrepresented, cursed, vilified, denounced, and libeled. Yet, it was by far the most fascinating part of my life."

Reagan considered *Kings Row* one of his best pictures. His costar, Bob Cummings, in that movie commented at the time, "Someday, I'm going to vote for this fellow for president." Even then, Reagan was talking about politics on his movie sets.

As World War II was coming to a close, Reagan's unit received secret footage from cameramen covering Hitler's death camps, revealing the inhumane treatment of the Jews during the Holocaust. Dutch was stunned and horrified by what he saw. He felt revulsion at seeing the tortured and malnourished bodies. He couldn't choke back the tears. It was something he would never forget.

When the Roach Studios were closed, Reagan kept a copy of the death camp film in case the validity of the Holocaust was ever challenged. He knew this documentary film would be solid proof. In fact, a documentary of these facts appeared in American movie theatres in April of 1945, called *The Nazi Murder Mills*. Throughout his political career, critics accused Ronald Reagan of confusing reality with unreality with regard to many movies made about World War II.

Would he be able to resume his movie career after the war?

A family portrait taken of Jack Reagan, Neil Reagan, Ronald Reagan, and Nelle Reagan for a family Christmas card around 1916–1917.

Ronald Reagan's birthplace in Tampico, Illinois, on February 6, 1911 in the apartment above the bank, which was a bakery at the time.

The Reagans moved to 104 Glassburn St. in Tampico when Dutch Reagan turned three months old.

In front of the Reagan house in Tampico was
Memorial Park, renamed Reagan Park.

Ronald Reagan learned to swim in the Hennepin Feeder
Canal just outside Tampico.

At 1219 Kellogg St. in Galesburg, Illinois, Dutch Reagan learned to read at the age of five. He discovered a collection of butterflies and birds' nests in the attic of this rental home.

Here in Monmouth, Illinois, the Reagans moved to a more modest home.

Here is the Memorial Arch for World War I in Dixon,
Illinois, where the Reagans lived for ten years.

This was one of five homes that the Reagans rented in Dixon at 816 South Hennepin Ave. It has become a national, historic landmark as Reagan's boyhood home.

Donald Reagan
"Dutch"
"Life is just one grand sweet song, so start the music"
President of Northside Student Body; Drama Club Pres.;
Football; Annual Staff; Hi-Y; Art; Lit. Contest; Track.

Ronald Reagan's senior high school picture in the *Dixonian* yearbook. His first name was misspelled.

Reagan as a lifeguard
at Lowell Park in
Dixon, Illinois, where
he saved 77 people.

Here is the famous Rock River in Dixon's Lowell Park, where Ronald Reagan was a lifeguard and saved 77 lives.

Hamburgers and root beer were sold at this bathhouse in Lowell Park right behind Reagan's lifeguard chair.

The Cement Works in Dixon employed many residents.
Dutch's father ran the Fashion Boot Store.

This Historic Center, named for Ronald Reagan, was
a school that Dutch attended in 6th grade. It became Southside
High School, where brother Neil attended. Dutch went
to Northside High School after they moved across
Rock River.

There is a portrait of Reagan inside made of 14,000 jellybeans.

Eureka College in Eureka, Illinois was a Christian College, where Reagan washed dishes, coached swimming, and played football to earn his tuition for four years.

The Chapel at Eureka where Reagan gave his first political speech as a freshman.

Dutch Reagan was transferred to the sister station WHO in Des Moines, Iowa, as a sports announcer.

A family photo taken in 1960 of Ronald Reagan, son Ron, Nancy, and daughter Patti outside their Pacific Palisades home in California.

President Reagan hugging Nancy Reagan at Rancho del Cielo
in Santa Barbara, California, on August 13, 1983.

President Reagan and Soviet General Secretary Gorbachev signing the INF Treaty in the East Room of the White House on December 8, 1987.

President Reagan gave a famous speech at the Berlin Wall, Brandenburg Gate, Federal Republic of Germany on December 12, 1987. "Mr. Gorbachev, tear down this wall!"

The Ronald Reagan Presidential Library in Simi Valley, California, where Presient Reagan was laid to rest after his death on June 5, 2004.

Outside the entrance to his presidential library, there is a bronze statue of President Reagan in his western riding clothes.

An Intermediate Range Missile is displayed inside President Reagan's Presidential library.

An authentic slab from the Berlin Wall stands outside the Ronald Reagan Presidential Library in Simi Valley.

12

The Screen Actors Guild and Nancy

By 1945, the wars in Europe and Asia were ended. Harry S. Truman succeeded Franklin Roosevelt as president when he died in office. Pakistan would declare independence from India in 1947. Wisconsin Senator Joseph McCarthy began his anti-Communist crusade in 1950 as the Korean War was starting. In 1952 General Dwight D. Eisenhower would be elected president to the first of two terms with Richard M. Nixon as his vice-president. Gamal Abdel Nasser became president of Egypt in 1954. Throughout the 1950s, the United States wrestled to establish racial integration on buses and in schools. In the late fifties, a young singer from Memphis, Tennessee, took the nation by storm. He was Elvis Presley.

During this time period, Ronald Reagan went back to his Hollywood routine of making films and providing for his family. He had joined the Screen Actors Guild (SAG) in 1941. After returning to civilian life, Reagan was thrust into the center of labor negotiations between rival unions in the film industry. A tough, honest negotiator, Ronald Reagan was made president of the Screen Actors Guild in 1947. Some of the forty-three unions were filled with communist members and sympathizers, who called Reagan a "one-man battalion," fighting against communism.

For years, Reagan spent his working hours on the movie set and his spare hours speaking at meetings or settling disputes. Although Reagan was still a liberal Democrat, he detested fascism and the possibility of communism destroying American values. He became a sought after speaker not only in the movie industry, but at the Chamber of Commerce and Rotary Clubs.

"As I look back now, I guess I was also beginning a political transformation that was born in an off-screen cauldron of deceit and subversion and a personal journey of discovery that would leave me with a growing distaste for big government," Reagan recalled.

Stars like Olivia de Havilland were determined to keep the film industry free of communist influence, and Reagan joined forces with her and others. The picket lines for stagehand and carpenter unions tried to keep their workers from crossing the lines and reporting for work. The lives of workers were threatened. Cars were bombed. It was a mild taste of terrorism. Reagan organized vans and buses to take the workers over the picket lines in safety. There were threats from thugs, who planned to throw acid in his face, intending to end his movie career.

With so many threats made against Reagan, the FBI insisted he wear a holster with a gun, and police were stationed outside his house for protection. There was very little time left for his family. When Jane Wyman filed for divorce in 1948, he was stunned and heartbroken. She was bored by his obsession with politics and the fact that he was never home. Besides, her career was moving forward. After her Academy award-winning performance as a deaf and dumb Mexican girl in *Johnny Belinda,* Jane Wyman was headed for stardom while Ronnie's career had reached a plateau. She also had lost a child (daughter Christina) in a premature birth. Ronnie moved into a small apartment in Beverly Hills and became a weekend parent. It was a painful and sad time for him.

To ease the pain of divorce, Reagan bought a ranch in the San Fernando Valley where he raised thoroughbred horses. When he was finally cast in a western, *Stallion Road,* after the war, he fell in love with a horse called "Baby" that belonged to an Italian horse-riding teacher. He persuaded Warner Brothers to let him ride the horse in the film and then he bought the horse from the Italian. Maureen and Michael had fun going out there in his red station wagon or spending the night at Nelle Reagan's, their grand-mother. Ronnie taught Michael how to ride and gave him a horse one Christmas. In fact, he taught all his children how to ride.

During the next four years, Ronald Reagan threw himself into his work as president of SAG or escaping to his ranch. The divorce from Jane had devastated him, and he cut himself off from the social scene.

In 1947 Ronnie testified against communism before the House Un-American Activities Committee. "I detest, I abhor their philosophy, but I detest more than that their tactics, which are those of the fifth column, and are dishonest, but at the same time I never as a citizen want to see our country become urged by either fear or resentment of this group that we ever compro-mise with any of our democratic principles through that fear or resentment…I still think that democracy can do it."

Many innocent actors, writers, and producers were wrong-fully blacklisted in that period. Reagan tried to defend them and to steer a middle course in all the proceedings. Reagan acknowledged that even his own career suffered from his strong opposition to communism. During this time of turmoil, he turned to politics and gave speeches for Democratic hopeful Harry Truman and Helen Gahagan Douglas against Richard Nixon in the senate race for California.

While Ronald Reagan was actively employed as a movie actor, he found himself in the 94% tax bracket and discovered that the Internal Revenue Service was taking a huge chunk of his money. This experience revolutionized his thinking about government. "The more government takes in taxes, the less incentive people have to work. Any system that penalizes success and accomplishment is wrong. Any system that discourages work, discourages productivity, discourages economic progress, is wrong. If you reduce tax rates and allow people to spend or save more of what they earn, they'll be more industrious; they'll have more incentive to work hard, and money they earn will add fuel to the great economic machine that energizes our national progress. The result: more prosperity for all—and more revenue for the government."

But his greatest source of joy was soon to come. Director Mervyn LeRoy called him one day in 1950 and said that a young actress named Nancy Davis needed help. There were several other actresses by the same name and one of them was accused of being a communist. She was afraid that false rumors and confusion over her name would associate her as a communist. Reagan told LeRoy that he would look into the matter. He found that this indeed was the case. He called LeRoy and asked him to tell Miss Davis that he would fix the situation, but Mervyn LeRoy felt Nancy Davis would not be satisfied because she was a "worrier" and why didn't Reagan take her to dinner to reassure her.

Reluctantly, Ronald Reagan agreed to meet her for a quick dinner to try to solve her problem. The dinner turned into a long evening. Reagan took her to hear singer Sophie Tucker sing into the wee hours. Eventually, their relationship turned into a long marriage. On March 4, 1952, Ronald Reagan and Nancy Davis had a quiet wedding with their best friends, actor Bill Holden and his wife Ardis, in attendance as best man and matron of honor. Their daughter Patti (Patricia Ann), was born later that same year. Their son, Ron, was born in 1958.

Financially, the newly married couple struggled to pay their bills. Nancy gave up her acting career to become a wife and mother. Ronnie decided not to take every part offered to him because he wanted more starring roles in better grade pictures. However, those parts weren't offered to him. Instead, they went to Las Vegas for two weeks for Ronnie to be the Master of Ceremonies for a variety act. They wanted him to stay longer, but Nancy and Ronnie wanted to go back to their new home that they had purchased in Pacific Palisades.

While Ronald Reagan's movie career was stalled, he was drawn more and more into politics, campaigning for Republican General Dwight D. Eisenhower for president and Richard M. Nixon as vice-president in 1952. His interest in the Democratic Party had faded since Hollywood's struggle against communism. Also, his high taxes left him very little money to support the ranch, his house, and his new family.

In the beginning, Reagan refused roles on television, thinking that a movie actor shouldn't make the crossover since it might endanger his career. Then in 1954, he was made an offer that he just couldn't refuse.

13

From Hosting TV to Politics

Many movie actors were suspicious of the future of television in the early days. Reagan was one of them.

Knowing how strongly Reagan felt about television for a movie actor, a friend, who oversaw television activities, approached him with an interesting idea. He said that the General Electric Company had decided to sponsor a weekly television program of high quality for an hour every Sunday evening, called the General Electric Theatre. There would be a different story every week with well-known actors in each teleplay. They wanted Ronald Reagan to be its weekly host. Because Ronnie would be playing himself and not a typecast character, he found the possibility fascinating. Besides, he needed the work. Ronald Reagan accepted the offer and began an eight-year association with General Electric.

Soon after Reagan became a successful host of the weekly program, the chairman of General Electric had an idea that he hoped Reagan would support. Because General Electric had 139 factories in 39 states, the chairman felt that these factories had a feeling of being separated from their home company. If Reagan could start visiting those plants, the workers might sense that the administration of GE cared about them. Ronald Reagan agreed. By bus and by train, he began a cross-country journey, greeting the workers, telling jokes, and sharing Hollywood stories with them. The factories loved these visits, which created a greater sense of loyalty to the company.

When rumors of Reagan's gift for giving speeches spread, he had many requests in the towns where these factories were located. After his meetings at the factories, people would come up to him afterwards and want to talk about issues of the day. With the chairman's approval, Ronald Reagan began talking about politics and they loved it. His standard speech lambasted government for interfering with business. Sometimes, he gave as many as fourteen political speeches a day about the evils of big government. He tried to make each speech different to avoid boredom and he wrote every single speech himself.

Despite Reagan's happiness during this period, a shadow of sorrow spread across his heart. His beloved mother contracted Alzheimer's disease in 1958. Ronnie and Nancy decided to put her in a nursing home, and she finally passed away in 1962. Because of Ronnie's special relationship to his mother, he was greatly saddened.

By the time 1962 arrived, Ronald Reagan had clocked in eight years with GE. However, the leadership at the top of the company changed. They no longer wanted Reagan to give speeches on their behalf. They wanted him to go on the road and sell their products. This was unacceptable to him. Ronald Reagan refused to become a salesman and the General Electric Theatre was canceled.

Reagan went back to what he knew best—movies. In 1964 he was offered the part of a villain in the final film (53 in total) of his career, *The Killers*. He also played host to a series called *Death Valley Days*. His movie career ended on a down note, but he realized why he had always been cast as the good guy. His fans could never accept him in anything but a positive role.

The 1960s were full of ups and downs. The country agonized over the Vietnam War as well as race riots. University campuses were aflame with violent protests against the war. Ronald Reagan campaigned for Richard Nixon in the 1960 presidential race against Senator John F. Kennedy although he had opposed Nixon during earlier days in California. John F. Kennedy was elected president, but would be assassinated while campaigning in Dallas in 1963. African American leader, Martin Luther King, Jr., would deliver his famous speech, "I have a Dream" in 1962, but he, too, would be assassinated in 1968. Britain's Winston Churchill died in 1965 while Indira Gandhi was elected prime minister of India in 1966. The communist Cultural Revolution gripped China in 1966. The Six Day War against Israel was waged and lost by the bordering countries to Israel in 1967.

Nancy and Ronald Reagan settled back into life in their home in the desirable Pacific Palisades area and commuted to their small ranch in Lake Malibu. Here, Reagan bred horses, built fences, and cleared trees.

But Ronald Reagan was undergoing a change in his political philosophy. His negotiating skills at SAG and eight years of giving speeches for GE shifted his viewpoint from liberal to conservative. By 1962 he registered as a Republican. When Barry Goldwater ran as a Republican presidential candidate in 1964 against Lyndon B. Johnson, Ronald Reagan was asked to make a televised speech, supporting Goldwater. It was a smashing success, especially his final words. "You and I have a rendezvous with destiny. We will preserve for our children this, the last best hope of man on earth, or we will sentence them to take the last step into a thousand years of darkness." People from all political parties found his words persuasive, but not enough to defeat Lyndon Johnson.

However, prominent Republicans were impressed. Several of them approached Reagan in 1964 to see if he would run for Governor of California to defeat the two term Democratic governor, Edmund (Pat) Brown. Ronald Reagan laughed. "I'm an actor, not a politician. I'm in show business." Still, they wouldn't take "no" for an answer. Ronnie and Nancy spent many sleepless nights over this request. He finally made the Republicans a proposal: he would talk to nonpolitical groups across California and find out what they were thinking and to see if they would come up with another candidate for governor.

Reagan discovered that he liked campaigning. Many journalists assumed that speeches were written for him and that he didn't have the intellect to write them himself. Reagan found a way to dismiss that accusation by conducting a question and answer period after his opening remarks. That way he would show the spontaneity and originality in answering any question. His speech for the Republican convention became known as "The Speech" or "A Time for Choosing," which Reagan wrote and rewrote for the campaign trail.

Inevitably, the public would ask him about his views of student protests on university campuses against the Vietnam War. He said, "The students had no business being at the university if they weren't willing to abide by the rules; if they refused to obey them, they should go somewhere else." There were cheers and standing ovations.

On Election Day in 1966, the political sparks were flying. By midnight the people of California decided that they wanted Ronald Reagan as their governor. He was elected by a landslide vote of one million over his opponent.

The celebratory breakfast began at the Coconut Grove in the Ambassador Hotel in Los Angeles. When Governor-elect Reagan strode into the room, his supporters cheered and roared their approval. They chanted, "Reagan! Reagan! Reagan!" Nancy was holding Ronnie's arm on one side and Mayor Sam Yorty (a Democrat) on the other. Moon Reagan, now employed by an advertising agency in Los Angeles, joined his brother at the center table.

The political honeymoon had begun.

14

California Chooses an Actor for Governor

The 1960s and 1970s were an emotional time for America.

During Reagan's two terms as governor from 1967 to 1974, the United States continued to be deeply involved in the Vietnam War. Richard M. Nixon would become a Republican president in 1968. After Nasser's death in 1970, Anwar Sadat became president of Egypt. China was admitted to the United Nations in 1971. President Nixon made a historic visit to China in 1972 to open relations between the two countries. Watergate, a scandal of spying and deceit against the Democratic Party in the Watergate apartment complex in D.C., swirled around the Nixon administration in 1973, forcing President Nixon to resign in 1974. Gerald Ford succeeded him as president.

During the Nixon years, Ronald Reagan, still governor of California, was asked by the president to take four trips abroad to eighteen countries in Europe and Asia as a goodwill ambassador. This gave Reagan an opportunity to meet and talk with the heads of many nations, giving him invaluable experience for his future election to the presidency. Nixon encouraged him to take his wife and children. When the children weren't in school, the Reagans included them in this opportunity.

The Reagans would soon be moving to Sacramento, the capitol of California, set in the hot central valley with Lake Tahoe and Yosemite National Park only a few hours away. Settled in 1849, Sacramento was famous for the gold rush days, the Pony Express, and where the first continental railroad began. It became the state capitol in 1854. Amid the trees and parkland, the picturesque American and Sacramento Rivers meet. A dozen universities surround the area.

It was a difficult move for Nancy and Ronnie to leave their house in the Palisades. Nancy decided that the Governor's Mansion was not right for them because the mansion needed a great deal of work, was too close to the street, and wasn't suited to their son's school needs. Republicans bought another house for them, which they rented to the Reagans for eight years and then sold for a profit. Patti was in boarding school in Arizona. Even at the age of fourteen, Patti was a rebel. Her liberal views made her unhappy that her father would be a conservative governor of California. The Reagans also would miss the hills and peace of their ranch, which they put on the market to sell. Nancy was not treated favorably in the press and she never felt comfortable in Sacramento. Friends were difficult to cultivate in the new environment.

After the election, Ronald Reagan had two months to prepare himself for being governor. Although Reagan had no political experience, he had promised the people of California, "We are going to squeeze and cut and trim until we reduce the cost of government. It won't be easy and it won't be pleasant."

His first priorities were to appoint an executive board to investigate how all the government agencies could be run more efficiently and secondly, to get the best qualified people into his cabinet. Reagan had his own philosophy of governing, "I don't believe a chief executive should supervise every detail of what goes on in his organization. The chief executive should set broad policy and general ground rules, tell people what he or she wants them to do, then let them do it; he should make himself (or herself) available, so that the members of his team can come to him if there is a problem. If there is, you can work it out together and, if necessary, fine-tune the policies. But I don't think a chief executive should peer constantly over the shoulders of the people who are in charge of a project and tell them every few minutes what to do."

His critics called Reagan's style of governing, "hands off." Reagan didn't mind this description of him because he didn't want to get embroiled in the details. He wanted to keep a broader vision. At the same time, he was a great reader and did read many of the memos and briefing books given to him. He didn't mind being underestimated either in California or Washington, D.C.

During Reagan's first year, 7,000 bills were proposed. He had to pick and choose the bills he really wanted to pass. With a sense of drama, he made a media splash with the passage of his first bill. Photographers squeezed into his office snapping pictures for their newspapers and magazines. In that first year, Governor Reagan passed 1,700 bills.

After a number of months in office, Governor Reagan appointed a new financial director, Caspar Weinberger, a San Francisco lawyer who came in 1968 and left in 1970. Immediately, Weinberger found a $200 million budget deficit and told the governor a million dollars was being spent every day. Thus, began the unpleasant task of cutting and trimming.

At the beginning of his first term, Reagan had to impose a 10% budget cut on all agencies. He put a hold on hiring and stopped buying new cars and trucks. He sold the former governor's private airplane.

Reagan's 57th birthday came in the middle of these cuts. His staff gave him a surprise party with an enormous cake that they wheeled into his office. Ten percent of the cake was missing to symbolize what he had to do in the months ahead. Reagan loved the humor and shared the cake with all his colleagues.

Next, he had to try and win over the Democratic Party's legislators. This strategy began by trying to persuade the chairman of the assembly, Jesse Unruh, to come around to Reagan's viewpoint. Unruh had no intention of departing from his ideals. He was a partisan politician and a big spender.

Unruh was a colorful character and the picture of an old time politician—a big, burly character, nicknamed "Big Daddy." His statement "money is the mother's milk of politics" was legendary. Unruh was a poor boy from Oklahoma and hitchhiked to California. He was hired by Lockheed and soon became a skilled union organizer. Socially, Reagan won Unruh over by telling an endless repertoire of jokes. Politically, Unruh was a solid wall.

At his first cabinet meeting, Ronald Reagan made this statement, "When I have a decision to make, I want to hear all sides of the issue, but there is one thing I don't want—political ramifications. The only consideration I want to hear is whether it is good or bad for the people."

One of his closest personal aides both as governor and president was Michael Deaver, a skilled public relations man. His motive was to help Ronald Reagan in every way he could.

Befriending First Lady Nancy Reagan was his top priority. Mrs. Reagan gave sound advice to Deaver, which he recalled in his book, *A Different Drummer,* "If I said that going to a certain event or supporting a certain bill would mean 'political death' for him, he would dismiss my argument out of hand. But if I said that his support of this bill or his attendance at this event would hurt people, Reagan would demand to know more and usually take my side if I could prove my case."

For example, Governor Reagan was concerned about the race riots in a section of Los Angeles called Watts. Reagan decided to visit the area secretly to find out what the causes were. He visited African/American and Hispanic families, asking them questions. Among many things, he found out that blacks were discriminated against during hiring in the state government and that children who spoke only Spanish were sent to schools for the retarded. When Reagan returned, he corrected these issues.

Stealing away secretly on some good deed would become a habit with the governor and even as president. If someone were in need, he would sit down and write them a personal check. If a soldier's wife didn't hear from her husband on their anniversary, he would go out and buy red roses, take them to her, and arrange for a telephone call. He never sought publicity or recognition for these humanitarian missions. He was following his mother's influence in performing charitable deeds.

In the first couple of months into his governorship, Reagan was invited to give the graduation speech at Chico University in the northern valley of Sacramento. No one wanted to go with him on that Saturday. Finally, Jack Lindsey, his Legislative Secretary, volunteered.

After the speech was over, the two men strolled over to the county fair. This county had strongly supported Reagan for governor and Lindsey thought it would be good to shake some hands to thank them.

While Reagan was chatting to people, Lindsey disappeared into a tent where they were auctioning off animals, raised by kids in the 4H Club. Lindsey spotted a little girl and her hog. He whispered in the auctioneer's ear that he should sell the little girl's hog to the man in the white cowboy hat for $250. Recognizing the newly elected governor, he agreed.

Lindsey joined Reagan, who was leaning on the fence around the corral, and told him to enter the bidding at $200. Reagan nodded. A spirited bidding began for the hog. At $250 everyone dropped out, except two people. It went back and forth, going higher and higher—not what Reagan and Lindsey had expected.

"Sold to the man in the white hat for $450!" Reagan waved and grinned broadly. The newspapers took a candid shot of Governor Reagan shaking the little girl's hand. Later, he sent her a personal check.

As they headed home, Reagan turned to Lindsey and said, "What am I going to do with that hog?"

"Give a ham and eggs breakfast for all the legislators," Lindsey replied.

Reagan thought this was a great idea and did give a breakfast, but not from the hog he purchased.

Another animal story happened when the California Horsemen's Association made a personal visit to the governor. They were hoping that open trails in the state would become law. Knowing how much Governor Reagan missed his horses, they offered to give him a horse during his years in Sacramento. Reagan was thrilled and told his staff.

Jack Lindsey cautioned the governor and asked how much the horse was worth.

"About $5,000," replied the governor.

"Worth the same amount as the vicuna coat," said Lindsey. "Remember when President Eisenhower's chief of staff, Sherman Adams, accepted the gift of a vicuna coat and had to resign because of the scandal?"

Reagan's face turned red with anger momentarily. He looked at the floor and then looked up and said, "I guess I better not accept the horse."

Turning to more serious matters, Reagan had to do something about Weinberger's discovery that California was almost broke. Swallowing his pride, Reagan was determined to go to the people and say that he had to make a small tax increase. He promised to return this money to the people as soon as he could. In fact, he had to make tax increases four times during his two terms.

Near the end of 1968, Weinberger informed him that there would be a budget surplus of $100 million for the next year. Reagan was ecstatic. Weinberger asked him how he wanted to spend it, but Reagan insisted that he wanted to give it back to the people as he promised. He swore Weinberger to secrecy. Instead of informing the legislature, Reagan went directly to the people on television, telling them the money would go to them as a tax rebate (one of four rebates during his two terms). He told the people to deduct 10% from their taxes and that would be their rebate. Californians were thrilled, but the Democratic legislature was furious.

Another huge saving came from the automobile renewal forms. Before the postal rates went up, the state sent out renewal forms, saving $200,000. The people cheered. This was something they could understand because it affected them personally.

However, there was one piece of legislation that he regretted. It was the relaxation of the abortion law. Another disappointment was the reaction of blacks and Hispanics to his hiring policies in state government. These racial minorities still did not believe him and requested a meeting with him in the governor's office. When they arrived, he told them how his mother had taught him about the evils of prejudice. He asked them why they didn't know that he had hired more minorities than any other governor. They didn't and asked him why he didn't brag about it. Ronald Reagan replied, "In appointing these people, I just was doing what I thought was right. I think it would have been cheap politics if I'd gone out and started singing a song about it. Besides, they were the best people for the job; I didn't appoint them because they were blacks…" The group was satisfied.

On social occasions, legislators and friends were eager to be invited to the Reagan's Sacramento home. In the basement was a huge toy train system set up for young Ron. It was laid out on an enormous table. Grown men became boys when they were shown the trains. Many of them spent much of a social evening playing in the basement with the trains. Upstairs, the guests could hear the hearty laughter booming from below.

In 1968 Ronald Reagan would be offered a new idea for his political life. Some Republicans came to him and asked him to run for president as a favorite-son. He told them he did not want to run for the presidency, but they assured him he would only be a favorite-son candidate and would lead the delegation at the convention and nothing more. He agreed, although many wanted him to run as a real candidate. In looking back, Reagan was relieved that he didn't run at that time. He conceded that he wasn't ready. Besides, he wanted to run for a second term as governor to finish some of the programs that he had started.

Did Californians want him for a second term?

15

Another Four Years in Sacramento

Governor Reagan liked holding political office. Political fever was now in his blood. He felt that he hadn't achieved all he wanted in his first term. It would take another four years to complete his agenda.

Ronald Reagan's Democratic opponent for that second term was none other than Jesse Unruh—the power broker for the Democratic Party in California. The margin of victory was far less than his first term. Reagan won by a margin of 53%, but large enough to give him a mandate to continue his policies. His second term concentrated on making and passing a fair welfare reform bill, known as the California Welfare Reform Act (CWRA). The abuse of the welfare program disturbed him greatly. He discovered fraud among a number of "welfare queens" who assumed many aliases and applied for welfare for children that didn't exist. In exchange for state money, welfare recipients were required to perform some kind of work. Poor people without children participated in a Community Work program that saved $2 billion.

Governor Reagan's weakest interest was in environmental issues. He was not overly concerned about saving forests and the Redwood Trees. On the other hand, he was concerned about holding property taxes down. So was Jesse Unruh, but neither

Reagan nor Unruh was able to reduce these taxes until Reagan left office. Proposition #13 was passed in 1978.

In an effort to make a change in public policy, Reagan always found that if he went directly to the people with his requests, it saved him endless conflicts with the state senate or assembly, which infuriated Jesse Unruh and the Democrats. Through television speeches, he told how the welfare system was being misused and encouraged the people to write to their representatives to correct it. The new chairman of the assembly complained to Reagan about his plan because they were swamped with postcards and letters. Reagan told him, "Sit down, we're all partners in this. Let's put aside our personal feelings and jointly go to work and see what we can get done." They did. They cut millions in expenditures.

Michael Deaver made some close-up observations of the man he watched over three decades. "His mannerisms were endearing. He was genuine and a good listener, not typical traits for a politician. He was charming, but it was a boyish charm, almost a naive posture that disarmed you…just when you were about to dismiss him, he'd answer a question with such eloquence, you were spellbound."

During the early years in Sacramento, Ronald Reagan was trying to break his smoking habit. Every time he was tempted to reach for a cigarette, he reached for a handful of jellybeans in a bowl on his desk. He especially liked the small ones called "jellie bellies." The jellybeans were for colleagues and guests, too. This addiction to jellybeans carried over into the Oval Office where a bowl was always on his desk.

After Ronald Reagan finished his eight years as Governor, he and Nancy started looking for a larger ranch for possible retirement. North of Santa Barbara and high in the Santa Ynez mountain range, they found 688 acres of breathtaking, unspoiled beauty. The drive up there was over seven miles of winding roads to the top. Once there, the land opened up to a sunny meadow, a lake, and a small 1872, white stucco, Mexican adobe house, which captured their hearts. It was a "Rancho del Cielo," meaning a ranch in the sky in Spanish, where they could have horses and dogs and ride over dozens of trails. The ranch became a retreat for building fences, chopping trees, and a place to think. They bought it in 1974. Thus began a major renovation by Ronald Reagan and two helpers that expanded the adobe house to more livable quarters for the Reagans, their family, and friends. They tried to have Thanksgiving there as often as possible.

At the age of sixty-five, Ronald Reagan still felt vigorous and useful. Besides working on the ranch, Michael Deaver, who had helped him run for governor and had a lively Public Relations firm, found speaking engagements for him. Reagan also started writing a weekly newspaper column as well as speaking for a radio spot. Life was never dull.

Whenever Reagan had a problem or something that he had to think through, he would mount his horse "Baby" or "Little Man" and go for a long ride. "There's something about the wild scenery and serenity at the ranch and having a horse between my knees that makes it easier to sort out a problem. I think people who haven't tried it might be surprised at how easily your thoughts can come together when you're on the back of a horse riding with nothing else to do but think about a decision that's ahead of you," Reagan said.

By the spring of 1975, Ronald Reagan had to take one of those long horse rides to make a critical decision. People, not politicians, kept calling him from all over the country, coaxing him to run against Gerald Ford for the Republican nominee for president in the 1976 election. After much thought, he agreed.

His decision was based on his disillusionment with the federal government in Washington. He felt it was just too BIG. Here are some of his reasons: "We had strayed a great distance from our founding fathers' vision of America. They regarded the central government's responsibility as that of providing national security, protecting our democratic freedoms, and limiting the government's intrusion into our lives—in sum, the protection of life, liberty, and the pursuit of happiness. They never envisioned vast agencies in Washington telling farmers what to plant, our teachers what to teach, our industries what to build. The Constitution they wrote established sovereign states, not administrative districts of the federal government. They believed in keeping government as close as possible to the people; if parents didn't like the way their schools were being run, they could throw out the Board of Education…"

Reagan relied upon his campaign team from his governor days to start organizing with one restriction—they had to abide by the eleventh commandment in which personal attacks were not to be made against his Republican opponents. Reagan didn't do as well as expected, especially in New Hampshire. His organizers insisted he leave on the eve of the primary to go to Illinois. That was a mistake. The people of New Hampshire felt slighted. At the Republican convention, Reagan lacked seventy votes to win his Party's nomination. Gerald Ford was the winner. Ford flirted with the idea of having Reagan for his vice-president, but

Ronnie had no interest although he encouraged Republicans to support Ford as he intended to do. In the national election, Governor Jimmy Carter, a Democrat from Georgia, defeated Gerald Ford.

But politics was still in Ronald Reagan's blood. After running for president against Ford in 1976, he knew that the desire to be president was something he now wanted, only if the American people wanted him to run.

16

America Wanted Reagan for President

Although Ronald Reagan returned to the lecture circuit and continued to write columns and speak on radio, Republican organizers approached him again in 1978 to see if he would let them start a campaign offensive for the 1980 election to defeat President Jimmy Carter and his vice-president, Walter Mondale. He gave them the go ahead.

During those early days of launching Reagan's campaign, John Sears was the manager. There seemed to be so much friction between Sears and the rest of his advisers that Reagan had to call them together to discuss the situation. In a rare move for Ronald Reagan, he fired the top three people and brought back his trusted colleagues—Bill Casey, Mike Deaver, Ed Meese III, and Lyn Nofziger.

There would be other Republican contenders for the 1980 race, including George H. W. Bush. When all of the nominees met in Nashua, New Hampshire, for a debate, no one wanted to share the cost. Therefore, Ronald Reagan agreed to pay for the televised debate and he included all the nominees. George Bush wanted a debate with only Reagan. At one point, the journalist host from the Nashua newspaper told Reagan to turn off his microphone. The genial Reagan suddenly was roused by anger and said, "I'm paying for this microphone!" The audience burst into applause. They saw that he could be a man of steel on matters of principle.

After Ronald Reagan won the Republican nomination at the convention, he was faced with making a choice for his vice-presidential running mate. Behind closed doors, Reagan and his advisers weighed the possibility of getting Gerald Ford to take the second slot. Ford's group would agree only on condition that Ford be a co-president. Both Reagan and Ford thought this was not a good idea, and Ford withdrew his name. Reagan immediately turned to George Bush as the most likely candidate. Bush accepted.

In the final days before the election, Reagan and Jimmy Carter held a final debate. Every time Carter would misstate Reagan's views, Ronald Reagan would shake his head and say, "There you go again." This phrase and the tough stand he took in New Hampshire seemed to sway the voters, giving Reagan the lead in the election poles.

The nickname for Ronald Reagan by the press became the Great Communicator. From his years as a sportscaster, actor, and governor, Reagan had polished his speaking skills. He could charm an audience of workers or diplomats or average Americans in person, on television, or over the radio. That husky voice appealed to the listeners. He was also nicknamed the "Teflon President" because nothing seemed to stick to him in the way of criticism or difficulties.

In fact, Nancy Reagan also referred to her husband's optimism in her book *My Turn*, "It can be difficult to live with somebody so relentlessly upbeat. There were times when his optimism made me angry...I longed for him to show at least a little anxiety. Ronnie doesn't worry at all. I seem to do the worrying for both of us."

On the eve of Ronald Reagan's election victory over Jimmy Carter in November of 1980, double rainbows appeared over Reagan's birthplace in Tampico, Illinois, after a late afternoon storm. To the residents, those two rainbows symbolized two terms for their native son.

During the time between the election and inauguration, Reagan and his team worked on a plan to reduce high inflation, high interest rates of 21.5%, and unemployment. Within a few days of taking office, Reagan removed price controls on oil and gasoline. He believed that fixed prices were not necessary and actually inhibited economic growth. Interest rates began to drop and so did oil and gas prices.

In January of 1981 when Ronald Reagan was inaugurated as the fortieth president of the United State, he and Nancy moved into the gracious White House. For eight years they would enjoy the pink cherry blossoms each spring, the many visitors at their state dinners, and the quiet family quarters that Nancy decorated with her yellow sofas from California. The president even had an exercise room where he would work out every day. According to his son Michael, he could do impressive chin-ups well into his seventies.

By lunchtime, after Ronald Reagan officially became president, fifty-two American hostages held in Iran 444 days were released. President Jimmy Carter had tried courageously, but unsuccessfully, to obtain their release. Ronald Reagan was particularly compassionate towards Carter on this sensitive issue and publicly acknowledged Carter's long efforts in trying to secure their release.

President Reagan felt very comfortable in the Oval Office. His duties and days seemed similar to those as Governor of California, except on a larger scale. One of the first orders of business was to make friends with the Democrats in Congress to win them over in helping him to pass legislation. He invited Tip O'Neill, Speaker of the House, and his wife to the private quarters of the White House for dinner. Fellow Irishmen, O'Neill and Reagan swapped stories and became friendly. However, the Speaker made it very clear that they were political enemies and he would not give up his partisan ideals.

Reagan finally understood O'Neill, "Tip was an old-fashioned pol (politician): He could be sincere and friendly when he wanted to be, but when it came to the things he believed in, he could turn off his charm and friendship like a light switch and become as bloodthirsty as a piranha. He was a politician and a Democrat to his roots. Until six o'clock, I was the enemy and he never let me forget it. So, after a while, whenever I'd run into him, whatever time it was, I'd say, 'Look, Tip, I'm resetting my watch; it's six o'clock.'"

To begin the economic recovery, President Reagan proposed a $41.4 billion budget cut and a 30% tax cut over three years. Reaganomics was defined as cutting major spending in government and cutting taxes at a rate of 10% a year to stabilize currency. The Supply Side economics theory was to stimulate growth in the economy by reducing taxes. As he had done in California, President Reagan went directly to the people on television to tell them about his economic recovery program.

Only a few months into his presidency, Ronald Reagan would experience a near death incident. On March 30, 1981, President Reagan was giving a luncheon speech at the Hilton

Hotel in Washington, D. C. His subject was the country's need for a strong, military defense. After the speech was over, Reagan walked outside to his limousine, surrounded by Secret Service officers. He turned to wave to the crowd when a series of shots, sounding like firecrackers, splintered the air. There was a scuffle and Reagan's bodyguard threw the president inside the limousine while he landed on top of him. Reagan thought his rib had been broken and was stabbing his lung, cutting off air. Only later did he learn that a young man, John Hinckley, Jr., with mental problems, had tried to assassinate him. The bullet barely missed the President's heart. One of his Secret Service people was shot in the chest and his press secretary, James Brady, was shot in the head. Both men survived.

The President managed to walk into the George Washington University Hospital by himself, but soon was placed on a gurney, which was quickly wheeled into the emergency room. Mrs. Reagan was informed and rushed to his bedside. When she took his hand, he looked up at her and quoted a line from heavyweight champion boxer, Jack Dempsey (after he was knocked out by Gene Tunney), and said, "Honey, I forgot to duck."

Once the president was on the operating table, he joked, "I hope all you doctors are Republicans!" The doctor replied, "Today, we're all Republicans." Within two weeks, Ronald Reagan was back at the White House. During his time in the hospital, the rumors about his hair being dyed to hide his gray hair were put to rest. Ronald Reagan had never dyed his hair and was relieved when some gray strands began to show at the end of his term in office.

However, at that moment when Ronald Reagan hung between life and death, his thoughts turned to his wife, "Seeing

Nancy in the hospital gave me an enormous lift. As long as I live, I will never forget the thought that rushed into my head as I looked up into her face, 'I pray, I'll never have to face a day when she isn't there…of all the ways God has blessed me, giving her to me was the greatest—beyond anything I can ever hope to deserve.'" Often, Reagan stated that he couldn't imagine life without her.

After the assassination attempt, Ronald Reagan wrote in his diary, "Whatever happens now I owe my life to God and will try to serve him in every way I can."

In those early months and during much of Reagan's presidency, Nancy Reagan came under tremendous scrutiny and criticism from the press. She brought back many antiques, stored in warehouses that came from the days of George Washington and other presidents. Also, the White House china had many mismatched patterns for State dinners. From private donations and private gifts, Mrs. Reagan was able to redecorate with a new, elegant china pattern without costing the taxpayers anything. Somehow, this wasn't believed and the press attacked the First Lady again and again. The media particularly focused on her gowns and dresses, which were offered to her by famous designers to wear at no cost to the Reagans, but providing free advertisements for the designers. From that day forward, the Reagans always paid for Nancy's gowns.

Most First Ladies select an issue or a cause to which they devote their time and energies. After the china controversy was solved, Nancy's closest aides suggested that she support the anti-drug movement for young people. The phrase "just say NO to drugs" became her trademark and brought her favorable press coverage.

For the President and First Lady, the greatest disappointment was their loss of privacy. The White House became a virtual prison for them as it had for many presidents and their families. They longed to take a stroll down the street and do a little shopping. On Valentine's Day, President Reagan insisted on going to a shop to buy Nancy some cards. Against the wishes of the Secret Service, arrangements were made. The disruption to the storekeeper, his store, and the general public was enormous. The president knew he couldn't do that again. Even his visits to church were curbed for fear of another assassination attempt. The Reagans found relief at Rancho del Cielo or at Camp David—a government lodge, surrounded by 150 acres of woods and trails where the Reagans could walk freely. In the evenings they watched movies with staff and friends, sharing large bowls of popcorn. It became their great escape.

During his first term, President Reagan surrounded himself with a capable cabinet. General Alexander Haig was appointed secretary of state. Caspar Weinberger was named secretary of defense. James Baker III became chief of staff while Michael Deaver assisted him with scheduling. Baker had good connections in Congress and an excellent relationship with the press.

One of his most historic appointments was that of Sandra Day O'Connor from Arizona's Court of Appeals to the Supreme Court on July 7, 1981, as the first woman to become a Supreme Court Justice. Reagan found her forthright, honest, and capable.

Perhaps President Reagan's most ardent passion during his presidency was to stop the expansion of communism around the world. His encounter with communism in Hollywood as the president of the Screen Actors Guild had left an indelible imprint on his outlook of life. In the spring of 1981, the

Brezhnev Doctrine was disturbing to him because the Soviets pretended to support wars of liberation in South and Central America as well as Afghanistan. In actuality, they wanted to be the ruling presence in those areas.

The Russian ambassador to the United States, Anatoly Dobrynin, let Reagan know that his country might be interested in East-West talks over the control of nuclear arms. Reagan responded in a tough way. On the other hand, Reagan realized the necessity of working out this issue. Shortly after leaving the hospital, he decided to write a personal letter to the Soviet Union's president, Leonid Brezhnev, along these lines. Brezhnev sent a swift reply, blaming the United States for prolonging the Cold War. Reagan's plan was put on hold temporarily.

The next test of the new president's backbone and leadership came in August of 1981. The Professional Air Traffic Controllers Organization of 17,000 people threatened to go on strike for higher salaries. President Reagan stepped in and said they would lose their jobs if they didn't go back to work in 48 hours. It took two years to train new employees, but most of them did return to work. This was a victory for the president. Outside nations began to perceive Reagan as a president who meant what he said.

A sad moment for President and Mrs. Reagan was the assassination in October of Anwar Sadat, President of Egypt, who had declared his friendship for the United States in a visit to the new American president. The Reagans found him to be a man of warmth and integrity. His efforts for peace in the Middle East would be greatly missed.

At a speech to the National Press Club in November, President Reagan once again raised his continuing desire for

Arms Reduction. His communication with Leonid Brezhnev in April had failed. In the Press Club speech, he suggested that there should be an elimination of all intermediate-range nuclear force weapons in Europe. Also, Reagan called upon the Soviet Union to reduce stockpiles of long-range strategic nuclear weapons. He suggested a START (Strategic Arms Reduction Talks) program. He actually introduced the idea in a speech at Eureka College. All of this made front-page news, but reaching such a goal took a few more years.

On the economic front, Reagan was able to compromise on the tax cut. Instead of 30% over three years, he compromised at 25% over twenty-seven months. His Tax Reform bill would not be approved until 1986. In the Caribbean, Central and South America, Reagan worked with Bill Casey, head of the CIA, to help these regions economically to stall the communist influence.

It was a challenging first year for the president, but he planned to stay the course of "a new beginning" for the country.

In 1982 came the first casualty from his cabinet. Alexander Haig, who did not always agree with Ronald Reagan on foreign affairs, resigned as secretary of state. Reagan quickly replaced him with the quiet, but strong-minded George P. Shultz, a man of integrity and respect. He would be loyal to his president and implement his policies.

At the end of May, the United States and the Soviet Union announced Strategic Arms Talks. Reagan had at least moved the country forward in a small step. By November, Leonid Brezhnev died, succeeded by Yuri Andropov.

In other areas of foreign policy, the president would create a Middle East initiative, sending Marine troops to Beirut, Lebanon, in the middle of 1982.

The years 1983 and 1984 would become intense. At the 1983 State of the Union address, President Reagan put a serious freeze on government spending. There was a successful G7 economic summit in Williamsburg, Virginia, but attacks against America in foreign countries were increasing. In April the U.S. embassy in Beirut was bombed, leaving 32 killed. By October the Marine barracks in Beirut was hit by a suicide bomb terrorist attack, killing 241 Marines. The Soviets shot down a Korean passenger airliner (KAL 007) for straying into its territory on September 1, 1983.

One of the critical highlights of 1983 happened in March when President Reagan gave a speech to a group of evangelical ministers in Orlando, Florida. He described the Soviet Union as "the aggressive impulses of an evil empire." The words "Evil Empire" bounced around the world like wildfire and would be remembered throughout his presidency and beyond. Reagan knew what the reaction would be. Even though his wife thought the language was too strong, he said, "I wanted the Russians to know I understood their system and what it stood for."

Next came an unexpected event. On October 21, 1983, President Reagan, Secretary of State George Shultz, and Secretary of the Treasury Don Regan flew to Augusta, Georgia, for a weekend of golf at the Masters' prestigious Augusta National Golf Course. Amid the blooming azaleas, dogwoods, and autumn colors, they planned to relax and play golf. At 4:00 a.m. the president was awakened by a telephone call from the National Security Adviser, telling him of the invasion of the island of Grenada by Cuban communists, who were supported by the Soviet Union. The Organization of Caribbean States had asked the United States to intervene.

Since there were 800 American students attending St. George's University Medical School, Reagan reacted quickly. He ordered the Pentagon to prepare a rescue mission within 48 hours. Because Americans were still sensitive to the failure of the Vietnam War, Reagan insisted that the mission be kept secret. Despite Reagan's excellent personal and professional relationship with Prime Minister Margaret Thatcher of Great Britain, she was not pleased when she heard about the American invasion. Thatcher called President Reagan in an angry mood and expressed her displeasure over not being informed. He apologized and explained. The two leaders continued their special friendship.

Of the successful Grenada invasion, President Reagan said, "The people of Grenada greeted our soldiers much as the people of France and Italy welcomed out GIs after they liberated them from Nazism at the end of World War II...I probably never felt better during my presidency than I did that day."

At the beginning of 1984, Ronald Reagan was intent on pressing forward on relations with the Soviet Union, but Yuri Andropov died and Konstantin Chernenko took over the leadership of the Soviet Union. Every time Reagan tried to establish a relationship, the Soviet leaders seemed to die.

17

A Bumpy Second Term

The whole of 1984 would be a big one for President Reagan. It was an election year. Although Nancy wasn't eager for him to seek a second term, Ronald Reagan definitely wanted to finish his agenda for the country. Every time Reagan was asked a question about given a choice between national security and the deficit, he replied, "I'd have to come down on the side of national defense." Audiences roared with approval at his answer.

Democrats Walter Mondale and Geraldine Ferraro would be his opponents. Reagan knew that the Democrats would attack the age and senility factors since he was seventy-four. To take the wind out of their sails, he delivered a funny line in one of the final debates with Walter Mondale before the election. "I am not going to exploit for political purposes my opponent's youth and inexperience." Everyone laughed, even Mondale. Apparently the audience loved it, and perhaps it may have turned the election in his favor because the Reagan/Bush team won 59% of the vote.

In reflecting about the 1984 campaign, Reagan said, "In a campaign, I always like to act as if I'm one vote behind; overconfidence is a candidate's worst mistake. I knew anything can happen in an election campaign; it's just as well I did run scared, because in the view of many people, I nearly blew the whole race during my first debate with Mondale that fall."

Reagan's second term would have incredible highs and painful lows. Because of changes in personnel during the latter part of Reagan's second term, he was not served well. James Baker became secretary of the treasury and Don Regan slipped into the chief of staff role. Michael Deaver resigned over his personal problems. Since Reagan never liked to fire anyone and avoided personal conflicts, Nancy tried to protect her husband by influencing staff changes indirectly, making herself unpopular. The wrong people in powerful positions damaged the Reagan presidency badly throughout the second term. Although Reagan personally liked Don Regan because he was a jovial Irishman who swapped stories with him, Regan was isolated from the Congress and disliked the press. By the time Regan was forced to resign, President Reagan's public image was at an all time low. Senator Howard Baker had to take over as chief of staff at the tail end of Reagan's second term.

One of the other incredible lows happened in the first few months of Reagan's second term. He agreed to mark the fortieth anniversary of World War II in April of 1985 by accepting German Chancellor Helmut Kohl's invitation to lay a wreath at the Bitburg cemetery.

An almighty storm of criticism came from American Jews, the press, and fellow Republicans because Nazi SS men were buried there. Despite pleas from Nancy, Michael Deaver, and others not to go to Bitburg, President Reagan refused to back down. "The German soldiers were the enemy and part of the whole Nazi hate era. But we won and we killed those soldiers. What is wrong with saying, 'Let's never be enemies again'?"

Reagan wrote these words in his diary. American General Matthew Ridgway (a World War II hero) at 91-years-old offered to come to Bitburg and help Reagan lay the wreath. Ridgway said, "It was time to make peace." The president also visited an old concentration camp for Jews, Bergen-Belsen, to be even-handed during his visit to Germany.

Once the Bitburg furor subsided, President Reagan's major mission was dealing with the Russians in reducing nuclear arms. He wrote long, personal letters to each Russian leader: Leonid Brezhnev, Yuri Andropov, and Konstantin Chernenko, but these old men died before a dialogue could start. Not until 54-year-old Mikhail Gorbachev took office in March of 1985 did Reagan find someone receptive to his ideas. On November 16, 1985, Reagan and Gorbachev met in Geneva, Switzerland, for a summit conference. The two men sat alone in a lakeside villa beside a roaring fire, discussing these issues. They disagreed on Reagan's Strategic Defense Initiative (SDI—a shield against missiles), but they agreed to reduce nuclear arms by 50%.

Encouraged by the Geneva meeting, another summit was arranged where they met again at Reykjavik, Iceland, in October 1986. This time Gorbachev and Reagan sat in a home overlooking the Atlantic, hashing out their disagreements. Before touching on the nuclear aspects, Reagan wanted to know why divided Jewish families couldn't be reunited. Gorbachev listened and seemed receptive. Eventually Gorbachev did release many Jews after Reagan repeatedly prodded him. The next day, the United States and Soviet Union were making progress on reduction of arms and conventional forces. As the two leaders were wrapping up their agreements, Gorbachev suddenly said that none of this would be possible unless the United States gave up SDI. Reagan blew up in anger and declared, "The meeting is over." Again, Reagan showed that he was a man of backbone.

However, negotiations through the Secretary of State and Russian officials continued as "quiet diplomacy," but Reagan refused to budge on SDI. Fourteen months later in December of 1987, Reagan and Gorbachev signed the INF treaty (Intermediate-range Nuclear Forces, which had a range between 300 and 3,300 miles). In the agreement, the Russians dismantled and destroyed 1,500 nuclear warheads, their intermediate range missiles in Europe, and SS-20s. The U.S. agreed to destroy their Pershing II missiles, cruise missiles, and 400 warheads. Inspections to verify were part of the agreement, too. In a strange way, President Reagan and Mikhail Gorbachev became friends and ultimately respected each other. Ronald Reagan's mission against the "Evil Empire" was accomplished.

On his way to attend an economic summit of the G7 in Venice, Italy, in June of 1987, President Reagan accepted an invitation to speak outside the Brandenburg Gate, where the Berlin Wall had been built by the Soviets to divide West Germany from communist East Germany. Thousands attended the open-air event. In conclusion to his remarks he said, "General Secretary Gorbachev, if you seek peace, if you seek prosperity for the Soviet Union and Eastern Europe, if you seek liberalization: Come here to this gate! Mr. Gorbachev, open this gate! Mr. Gorbachev, tear down this wall!" This final sentence has been repeated again and again throughout the years.

When George H. W. Bush became the forty-first president in 1989, Gorbachev ordered the wall to be torn down. A slab from the wall can be seen at the Reagan Presidential Library in

California and in the Peace Garden at Eureka College. Looking through the glass entrance of the Library, one can see the eight or ten-foot slab planted in the garden, overlooking the distant hills. It is a reminder that no wall can withstand the power of freedom. In a small meditation garden at Eureka College, there is a bust of Ronald Reagan in the center. To one side is a two foot slab from the Berlin Wall with graffiti on it.

One of President Reagan's most heartbreaking moments was the explosion in midair of the spacecraft "The Challenger" on January of 1986. The death of 241 marines in a suicide bombing in Beirut, Lebanon, in 1983 was equally agonizing.

Perhaps the blackest mark and one of the most ruinous episodes in the Reagan presidency came to be known as the Iran-Contra affair. From the very beginning of his administration, President Reagan had been concerned about the communist influence in Central America. Grenada was a prime example. But he knew that the Russians were supplying Nicaragua and El Salvador with arms. The Monroe Doctrine of 1823 prevented outside interference in these areas. Reagan was convinced something had to be done.

Neither Congress nor the Democrats would listen to Reagan's warnings. In fact, the president lost his temper at Tip O'Neill in the Oval Office when O'Neill blocked Reagan's efforts in helping Central America. "The Sandinistas have openly proclaimed Communism in their country, and their support of Marxist revolutions throughout Central America…they're killing and torturing people! Now what the hell does Congress expect me to do about that?"

The Contras were the freedom fighters against the Sandinistas in Nicaragua. Since the Congress would not authorize money for arms supplies, Reagan had to think of another way and the Iran-Contra resulted.

The Iran-Contra is a complicated story. In 1985 the terrorists in Lebanon kidnapped more American hostages. Ronald Reagan longed to get these hostages released and back to their families. He didn't want to bargain with terrorists, but he wanted to find a way to free the hostages. The Israelis came to the Americans with an idea. According to them, there were moderates in Iran who wanted to introduce democracy to their country once the radical clerics were out of power. The Israelis felt that these Iranians could influence the terrorists in Lebanon to release the American hostages, which they finally did. The Israelis offered to sell arms and missiles to that moderate group in Iran. They then proposed that the Americans would replace those weapons by selling them to the Israelis. The CIA would then take the cash from that sale and give money for arms to the Contras in Nicaragua.

George Shultz and Caspar Weinberger advised the president against such a move, but Reagan ignored their advice and proceeded. Warnings by Shultz and Weinberger turned out to be right, but Admiral John Poindexter, National Security Adviser, and Oliver North, an ex-Marine on the National Security Council and staff member to Poindexter, secretly went forward with Reagan's wishes to gain the hostages' release.

In the aftermath, the apparent illegal exchange of arms for hostages brought an outcry from the American public, causing a long series of hearings that blackened Reagan's presidency. Reluctantly, he had to admit his responsibility in these wrong series of events. Reagan claimed that the NSC (National Security Counsel) did not keep him informed and had gone beyond his recommendations. The Reagan Presidential Library has two long bookshelves in the archives, devoted to those hearings. Yet, the upstairs display has only one small section of a wall, in which the Iran-Contra is mentioned.

18

The Long Farewell

The eight years of the Reagan presidency are remembered for their economic recovery, nuclear arms reduction, and the rescue of 800 American medical students on the island of Grenada in 1983. The biggest shadow cast over the Reagan presidency was the Iran-Contra affair.

Two staff appointments in 1987 saved the final days of the Reagan presidency. They were retired Senator Howard Baker to replace Don Regan as chief of staff and General Colin Powell as Reagan's sixth National Security Adviser. Powell's invaluable restraint in global areas was a positive influence on Reagan.

Both the Tower Commission in 1987 and later the public trial accused many Republicans in Reagan's administration of being involved in the Iran-Contra conspiracy. In the end, no one was punished. Reagan's motive to free the hostages was not questioned, but the means to achieve the release hurt his reputation.

Ronald Reagan was an optimistic man, who loved to tell jokes and stories. His Midwestern straight talking and sincerity drew leaders and friends to him from all over the world. Margaret Thatcher, Prime Minister of Great Britain, became a longtime friend and ally. Long after his removal from power, Gorbachev maintained his friendship with the Reagans.

Whether Reagan met a janitor or head of state, he was always the same person.

On his last day as President of the United States, Ronald Reagan walked back to the Oval Office—devoid of his papers and memorabilia—for one last look, one last memory, one last bit of nostalgia. As he and Nancy boarded the plane to take them back to California, he turned to her and grinned, saying. "Well, it's been a wonderful eight years. All in all, not bad—not bad at all." As the helicopter circled the White House for one last time, Reagan looked out and said, "Look, honey, there's our little bungalow."

Many people speculate how ex-Presidents can adjust to normal life after leaving the White House and after holding such a powerful position. Nancy Reagan answered that question in her book, *I Love You, Ronnie,* "Ronnie never had a problem changing from one phase of life to the other. I think that's because no matter what he's doing or where he is in the world, he is always the same. And as far as I was concerned, everything was always fine as long as he was there." She also said, "Ronnie is not a complicated man. What you see is what you get."

In July of 1989, the Reagans went to Mexico to visit friends. One morning Ronald Reagan rode horseback with several friends. On the way up a steep incline, his horse was frightened by a loud noise and began bucking uncontrollably. By the third time the horse bucked, Reagan was thrown from the horse and hit his head. The Secret Service people quickly had him airlifted to a hospital in Tucson, Arizona. Upon his release, the Secret Service advised President Reagan not to ride again even at his beloved ranch.

Once Reagan left office, he concentrated on writing his auto-biography and on the building of his presidential library on a hill—700 feet high—in Simi Valley, California, covering an area of 100 acres. Big and small rocks were embedded in the land and were removed by heavy trucks with eight gears. Many rodents and other small animals were displaced, but found homes elsewhere. Ronald Reagan took an active interest in its construction. From the 153,000 square foot, modern pink stucco building, there are distant views of the Sierra Madres, Santa Monica Mountains, and the Pacific Ocean on a clear day. It cost $64 million, funded from private donations, and was dedicated in 1991 with five living presidents in attendance.

The entrance is dramatic. A larger than life-size bronze statue of Ronald Reagan in his riding clothes and cowboy hat is outside the front doors. Through the glass doors and windows can be seen the tall slab from the Berlin Wall with the graffiti still scribbled on the concrete. There is a replica of the Oval Office, the cabinet room, the Reykjavik meeting room, and an intermediate-range nuclear missile. There are pictures of Dutch Reagan's boyhood and of Nancy Davis Reagan's childhood.

Ronald and Nancy Reagan were interested in every aspect and detail of the library. In the planning stage, the Reagans took a longtime friend, Doris Heller, to lunch to ask her to run the gift shop at the library. Reagan wanted her to travel to all the presidential libraries to observe how they were run. Doris Heller had been a fashion model in New York City and then became vice-president of Magnim's department store in Beverly Hills. She had known Nancy Reagan for quite a while.

Heller's memories of Ronald Reagan were poignant ones. "One time when I was visiting at the ranch after the attempted assassination, President Reagan brought out a box to show me. Inside was the bullet that had been taken out of him. He laughed about it," she said. "Once something was over, he let it go."

Nostalgically, she commented, "Ronald Reagan was such a boyish man. He was so natural and loved people…especially young people. They weren't impressed by who he was. He could tell who was real and who wasn't. He had such a great sense of humor and there was so much goodness about him, and he loved to surprise people."

"When I finally decided to leave the library after five years, they gave a big party for me. I'd been saving something to give President Reagan and that seemed the right moment. Somehow, someone had given me Ronald Reagan's first inaugural address, written on a yellow pad with scribbled edits and changes. I put it in my safe deposit box and this seemed the right time to give it to him. I had no idea how it came to me, but I wasn't interested in getting money for it. When I presented it to President Reagan, everyone was shocked. They took it from me and immediately put it in the vault," said Doris Heller with a broad smile.

In the arena of friendships, Ronald and Nancy Reagan were successful, but in family relationships, they were not always successful. All of the Reagan children, except Maureen, had relationship problems and philosophical differences with their parents from adolescence into adult years. Because Michael was adopted, he felt excluded. Patti was a free spirit; she differed with her father politically and was estranged from her mother.

However, in 1997 Nancy Reagan found a letter, written to her daughter in 1997 by her husband. He never sent it, but it pleaded with Patti to remember the good times and look at the family photo albums. His final words to her were, "Pictures don't lie." Nancy gave the letter to Patti, who began reflecting on her childhood and her years as a rebellious daughter.

When Patti Davis reconciled with her family, there was speculation that her father's disease was the reason. In her own words, Patti made this response, "I returned to my family, the prodigal child, in October 1994, two months before my father disclosed to the world that he had been diagnosed with Alzheimer's. It's been reported that his disease brought us back together. That's not quite true—it happened earlier, when my mother and I laid down the armaments of our long dispiriting war, allowing the rest of the family to breathe easier, drift toward one another. But the chronology doesn't really matter; the coming together does. I returned in time to say good-bye to my father, to witness his steady withdrawal from the world. During the last couple of years, I would sit beside my father, silence floating between us, knowing that we would never be anymore to each other than we were right then."

As Patti Davis matured, she became a respected novelist. Some of her early novels, however, exposed her anger against her parents and their political philosophy. Once she approached the age of fifty, her character underwent a transformation. She was filled with personal regrets over the pain that she had caused her parents, and her spiritual outlook deepened. Her beautifully written non-fiction book, *The Long Goodbye,* in 2004 chronicled her changing relationships to those closest to her, particularly her father. She learned to appreciate his qualities and the many life lessons he had taught her in her childhood.

One of the consistent descriptions of Ronald Reagan by his family and friends was his tendency to be remote or aloof or distant. Even his beloved Nancy had the same occasional complaint, "Although he loves people, he often seems remote, and he doesn't let anybody get too close. There's a wall around him. He lets me come closer than anyone else, but there are times when even I feel the barrier."

Michael Reagan's comment on this subject, "He can give his heart to the country, but he just finds it difficult to hug his own children." In his final years, Reagan always remembered Michael as the man who hugged him good-bye.

Son Ron Reagan regarded his father this way, "I had a friendly and loving relationship with my father, but you almost get the sense that he gets a little bit antsy if you try and get too close and too personal and too father-and-sonny. He really didn't have a role model himself for a father. So, what fathering he did, he had to come by on his own."

On November 5, 1994, Ronald Reagan wrote a letter to the American people, revealing his struggle with Alzheimer's. Here are some parts of this heartfelt letter.

"My Fellow Americans,

I have recently been told that I am one of millions of Americans who will be afflicted with Alzheimer's Disease.

…At the moment I feel fine. I intend to live the remainder of the years God gives me on this earth doing the things I have always done. I will continue to share life's journey with my beloved Nancy and my family. I plan to enjoy the great outdoors and stay in touch with my friends and supporters.

Unfortunately, as Alzheimer's Disease progresses, the family often bears a heavy burden. I only wish there were some way I could spare Nancy from this painful experience. When the time comes I am confident that with your help she will face it with faith and courage.

…I now begin the journey that will lead me into the sunset of my life. I know that for America there will always be a bright dawn ahead.

Thank you, my friends. May God always bless you.

Sincerely.

Ronald Reagan"

When one of the Secret Service men at the ranch heard the news, he broke down and cried. The cheerful man who greeted him every day with a joke or story couldn't remember any of the hundreds of anecdotes he had told him. In 1998 the Reagans sold their ranch to the Young America's Foundation. They had moved to a house on St. Cloud Drive in Bel-Air, California, overlooking the Pacific Ocean.

The bumpy relationships with some of his children were repaired. His son Michael had discovered the identity of his late birth mother and of a half-brother, who was seven years younger. Those discoveries gave him peace and made him grateful for his adoptive parents. He was even able to express love and gratitude to them. After finding his biological roots, Michael didn't feel like such an outsider. All this happened before Ronald Reagan's illness. Daughter Maureen Reagan had passed away in 2001 and always had a good relationship with her father and Nancy. Ultimately, however, Reagan didn't recognize anyone that he loved, even his beloved wife to whom he had written hundreds of love letters during their long years of marriage.

Even though Reagan's final ten years were a tragic conclusion to an otherwise star-studded career, Ronald Reagan's son, Ron, said that his father continued to be the same sweet-natured man, well into his nineties. Only the smile and shell of the fortieth president remained—still likable, still optimistic. Nancy Reagan wanted that view of her husband to remain in the public's mind. Patti Davis, too, felt that her father's soul existed despite the years of silence.

Unselfishly and uncomplainingly, Nancy Reagan became the final protector of her husband, sitting beside him during those long years. Her true reward came during the final moments of his life. He opened his blue eyes briefly and looked straight into her eyes. Ronald Reagan had always said that he wanted to see Nancy the first thing in the morning and the last thing at night. In his last moments on earth, he had eyes only for her and then he slipped into the great beyond. The speeches of praise for her husband over a week were another reward for Nancy Reagan. His place in history was assured.

In the long, sad farewell to Ronald Reagan, the American people expressed their respect and affection. His optimism for America was contagious. People believed in him because he truly believed in what he said. Because Ronald Reagan had pride in his country, so did the American people. Not only was Ronald Reagan the Great Communicator, he was a true patriot…ambitious for his country, not for himself. Perhaps it was the greatest role that he ever played.

Epilogue

Ronald Reagan had lived through World War I and World War II, the Korean War, the Vietnam War, and the Persian Gulf War. He was not aware of the Iraq War or the events of 9/11. During his lifetime, there were revolutionary changes in technology. The major economic depression of the 1930s deeply impacted his life and that of his parents. His own presidency led to major swings of prosperity in the 1980s and 1990s.

On June 5, 2004, Ronald Wilson Reagan passed away after a long journey through the heartbreak of Alzheimer's.

Despite his absence from the public eye during that decade from 1994 to 2004, an outpouring of affection and grief engulfed this country and many nations, upon hearing of his death. For more than a week, the American people seemed unable to let go of one of the most popular presidents of the twentieth century as well as the longest living president at the age of ninety-three.

A flood of condolences and eulogies, praising his qualities of decency, kindness, and optimism, came from both ordinary and extraordinary people. At the memorial service in the National Cathedral in Washington, D.C., words of commendation were spoken by former President George H.W. Bush (who served as Reagan's vice-president for eight years), Britain's former Prime Minister Margaret Thatcher, who delivered a taped tribute although she was present; President George W. Bush, and other dignitaries. Former President H.W. Bush was near tears when he described Ronald Reagan. He emphasized Reagan's special gift of kindness and said that he had learned much from him.

The most heart-wrenching scenes were those of the Reagan family, who seemed unable to come to grips with their loss. When Nancy Reagan stroked the coffin and laid her cheek against the shiny, wooden cover, she pressed her lips for a final kiss. The portrait of a devoted and adoring wife was a poignant moment. Instinctively, her son Ron and daughter Patti closed around her with Michael Reagan behind the trio. The Reagan family became unified in comforting their mother and step-mother.

As President Reagan was put to rest on the grounds of his presidential library in Simi Valley, California, the setting sun in the west spread its burnished golden rays across the hills. It symbolized the end of a life. Then, Nancy Reagan said her final good-byes to her husband of more than fifty years. The world said its final good-byes, too.

The Program of Ronald Reagan's Memorial Service
June 11, 2004 Washington National Cathedral

❖

CELEBRANT

The Reverend John C. Danforth

PARTICIPANTS

The Right Reverend John Bryson Chane
Bishop of Washington and Dean of the Cathedral

The Right Reverend A. Theodore Eastman
Vicar, Washington National Cathedral

His Eminence Angelo Cardinal Sodano
Secretary of State, Personal Representative of Pope John Paul II

His Eminence Theodore Cardinal McCarrick
Catholic Archbishop of Washington

His Eminence Archbishop Demetrios
Primate of the Greek Orthodox Church in America

Imam Mohamed Magid Ali
Imam and Director of the All Dulles Area Muslim Society

READERS

Rabbi Harold Kushner

The Honorable Sandra Day O'Connor

TRIBUTES

The President of the United States

The Honorable George H. W. Bush

The Right Honourable The Baroness Thatcher, L.G., O.M., F.R.S.

The Right Honourable Brian Mulroney

HONORARY PALL BEARERS

The Honorable Michael K. Deaver

Mr. Merv Griffin

Brigadier General John E. Hutton, MC U.S. Army, Retired

The Honorable Frederick J. Ryan, Jr.

The Honorable Charles Z. Wick

-2-

Some Memorable Quotes by Ronald Reagan

"There is no limit to what a man can do or where he can go if he doesn't mind who gets the credit." January 21, 1981.

"We have the right to dream heroic dreams. Those who say that we're in a time when there are no heroes, they just don't know where to look." January 20, 1981.

"In America, our origins matter less than our destination, and that is what democracy is all about." August 17, 1992.

"I've always believed that a lot of the trouble in the world would disappear if we were talking to each other instead of about each other." April 11, 1984.

"Whatever else history may say about me when I'm gone, I hope it will record that I appealed to your best hopes, not your worst fears; to your confidence rather than your doubts. My dream is that you will travel the road ahead with liberty's lamp guiding your steps and opportunity's arm steadying your way."

TIMELINE

1911   February 6: Ronald Wilson Reagan was born in Tampico, Illinois, to Nelle and Jack Reagan. His brother Neil was born in 1908.
First electric car by General Motors.

1916   National Park Service started.

1920   The family finally moved to Dixon, Illinois, after Chicago, Galesburg, Monmouth, and Tampico.

1921   Albert Einstein comes to New York City to talk about his Theory of Relativity.

1926   Worked as a lifeguard in Lowell Park.

1927   Telephone connection between New York and London.
Charles Lindbergh flies solo between New York and Paris.

1928   Graduated from Dixon's Northside High School, where he played football, track, basketball, and drama. Worked on yearbook and was student body president.

1929   First Academy Awards presented.

1932   Graduated from Eureka College where he played football and was on the swimming team while being student body president.

1933   Worked at radio stations WOC and WHO in Davenport and Des Moines, Iowa.

1935   Social Security started.

1937   Hollywood screen test with Warner Brothers, signed a seven-year contract. Also, he was promoted to Second Lieutenant in the Reserve Corps of Cavalry. *Love is on the Air* was his first motion picture.

1939   World War II began when Germany invaded Poland.
Films "Wizard of Oz" and "Gone with the Wind" produced.

1940   Married Jane Wyman after their work together on the *Brother Rat* film. Played George Gipp in *Knute Rockne-All American*.

1941   Maureen Reagan was born. He starred in *Kings Row*.
Jack Reagan, Ronald Reagan's father, died of a heart attack.
Japanese attack Pearl Harbor.

1942   Worked at Ft. Roach, making training films for the Army.

1945   Adopted Michael Reagan.
FDR dies. Harry Truman becomes president. Germany surrenders.
Japan surrenders.

1947   Elected President of the Screen Actors Guild. Testified before the
House Un-American Activities Committee.

1948   United States recognizes Israel.

1949   Ronald Reagan and Jane Wyman divorce.
North Atlantic Treaty Organization (NATO) formed; United Nations
dedicated.

1950   North Korea invades South Korea.

1952   March 4: Married Nancy Davis. Patricia Reagan was born.
Dwight Eisenhower becomes president.
King George VI of Great Britain dies and Elizabeth II becomes Queen.

1954   Host of the GE Theatre and spokesman for General Electric Company,
giving speeches across the country.
Senate condemns Joseph R. McCarthy.

1958   Son Ronald Prescott Reagan was born.1962 GE Theatre was canceled.
U.S. helps South Vietnam under John F. Kennedy's leadership.
Ronald Reagan's mother, Nelle, passes away.

1964   Reagan's speech for Barry Goldwater at the Republican convention,
which launched his own political career.
Dr. Martin Luther King wins Nobel Peace Prize.

1966   Elected Governor of California over Edmund G. (Pat) Brown.
Mao Tse Tung's Cultural Revolution begins in China.

1970   Won re-election as Governor of California over Jesse Unruh.

1975   Announced his candidacy for President of U.S. for the 1976 election.
Lost to incumbent Gerald R. Ford.
Margaret Thatcher elected first woman leader of Britain's
Conservative Party.

1979   Thatcher is elected the first woman prime minister of Great Britain.

1980   Reagan and Bush won the presidential election. Reagan was the 40th President.

1981   March 30: Assassination attempt.
July 7: Appointed Sandra Day O'Connor to the Supreme Court.
August 3: Air Traffic Controllers strike.
November 18: Arms Reduction speech to National Press Club.

1982   May 9: START/SALT II Speech at Eureka College.
May 31: Joint US-USSR announcement on Strategic Arms Reduction Talks.
June 25: George Shultz appointed Secretary of State.
November 10: Soviet leader Leonid Brezhnev dies.

1983   Federal spending freeze.
National Security and Strategic Defense Initiative (SDI) announced.
Suicide bomber in Beirut, Lebanon, kills 241 U.S. Marines.
Invasion of Grenada in October prevented communist take-over.

1984   Soviet leader Andropov dies and Konstantin Chernenko takes over.
Nuclear agreement with China.
G7 summit in London.
Reagan debates Walter Mondale as Democratic presidential candidate.
Prime Minister Indira Gandhi of India assassinated.
Reagan wins landslide victory for second term.

1985   Don Regan replaces James Baker as Chief of Staff; Baker becomes Secretary of the Treasury. Edwin Meese II becomes Attorney General.
Soviet Chernenko dies and Mikhail Gorbachev becomes leader.
Nicaraguan Peace Plan announced.
TWA flight 847 hijacked.
Economic sanctions against South Africa.
Geneva Summit with Gorbachev.

1986   Space shuttle *Challenger* explodes in midair.
Chernobyl nuclear reactor accident.
Summit in Reykjavik, Alaska, begins in October, but ends abruptly.
Iran-Contra scandal breaks and Tower Commission begins.1987 Don Regan replaced by Howard Baker. William Webster head of CIA.
Alan Greenspan made Chairman of Federal Reserve Board.

G7 summit in Venice lifted tariffs on Japan.
Berlin speech, "Tear down this wall, Mr. Gorbachev."
INF Treaty signed.

1988   Reagan endorses George H.W. Bush to run for president.
Addresses U.N. Assembly on disarmament.
Reagan's Presidential Library has groundbreaking.
Meets Gorbachev in NYC.

1989   Farewell address and George H. W. Bush inaugurated.

1990   Mikhail Gorbachev wins Nobel Peace Prize.

1991   Reagan Library opened.
Persian Gulf War.

1992   Bill Clinton defeats George Bush for president.

1993   Yitzhak Rabin of Israel and Palestinian Chairman Yassir Arafat met
and shook hands for peace on the White House grounds.

1994   Reagan diagnosed with Alzheimer's and tells the nation in.

1996   Neil Reagan dies

1998   The Ronald Reagan Washington National Airport renamed.

2001   Terrorists strike and destroy the Twin Towers in NYC.

2003   Iraq War begun under George W. Bush's presidency.

2004   June 5: Ronald W. Reagan passes away.

Bibliography

Books:

Angelo, Bonnie. *First Mothers*. New York. Harper Collins, 2000.

Cannon, Lou. *President Reagan: The Role of a Lifetime*. New York. Public Affairs,1991; 2001.

Cannon, Lou. *Governor Reagan*. New York. Public Affairs. 2003.

Daniel, Clifton. *Chronicle of the 20th Century*. Mount Kisco, New York. Chronicle Publications, 1987.

Deaver, Micahel K. *A Different Drummer*. New York. Harper Collins, 2001.

Morris, Edmund. *Dutch, A Memoir of Ronald Reagan*. New York. Modern Library, 1999.

Reagan, Michael E. *On the Outside Looking In*. New York. Zebra Books, 1988.

Reagan, Nancy. *I Love You, Ronnie*. New York. Random House, 2000.

Reagan, Ronald. *Ronald Reagan, An American Life*. New York. Pocket Books, 1990.

Reagan, Ronald. *Where's the Rest of Me?* Des Moines and New York. Meredith Press, 1965.

Wymbs, Norman E. *A Place to go Back to.* New York. Vantage Press, 1987.

Wymbs, Norman E. *Ronald Reagan's Crusade.* USA. Skyline Publications, 1996.

Magazines:

Newsweek, Commemorative Edition. Pages 22-45. June 14, 2004.

Time, Commemorative Issue. Pages 22-62. June 14, 2004.

Multimedia:

A&E Biography. *Ronald Reagan, A Role of a Lifetime. 1996.*

The Committee for the Reagan Trail has designed a visitor's map for going to all the towns in Illinois where the Reagan family moved: Tampico, Chicago, Galesburg, Monmouth, and Dixon. Eureka is also on the map.

Information was obtained by my personal visits to boyhood homes in Chicago, Dixon, Galesburg, Monmouth, and Tampico, Illinois. I researched archives at Eureka College, Illinois; visited Radio Stations WOC and WHO in Iowa as well as the Ronald Reagan Presidential Library in Simi Valley, California. Contacts and interviews were made in every town.

A List of Ronald Reagan's 53 Movies

1937   *Love is on the Air*

1938   *Hollywood Hotel*
        Swing Your Lady
        Sergeant Murphy
        Accidents Will Happen
        Cowboy from Brooklyn
        Boy Meets Girl
        Girls on Probation
        Brother Rat (with Jane Wyman)

1939   *Going Places*
        Secret Service of the Air
        Dark Victory
        Code of the Secret Service
        Naughty But Nice
        Hell's Kitchen
        Angels Wash Their Faces
        Smashing the Money Ring

1940   *Brother Rat and a Baby* (with Jane Wyman)
        An Angel from Texas (with Jane Wyman)
        Murder in the Air
        Knute Rockne-All American
        Tugboat Annie Sails Again (with Jane Wyman and Neil Reagan)
        Santa Fe Trail

1941   *The Bad Man*
        Million Dollar Baby
        Nine Lives Are Not Enough
        International Squadron

1942   *Kings Row*
        Juke Girl
        Desperate Journey

1943   *This is the Army*

1947   *Stallion Road*
        That Hagen Girl
        The Voice of the Turtle

1949   *John Loves Mary*
        Night Unto Night
        The Girl from Jones Beach
        It's a Great Feeling

1950   *The Hasty Heart*
        Louisa
        Storm Warning
        Bedtime for Bonzo

1951   *The Last Outpost*

1952   *Hong Kong*
        She's Working Her Way Through College
        The Winning Team

1953   *Tropic Zone*
        Law and Order

1954   *Prisoner of War*
        Cattle Queen of Montana

1955   *Tennessee's Partner*

1957   *Hellcats of the Navy* (with Nancy Davis)

1961   *The Young Doctors*

1964   *The Killers*

Index

0-595-33658-2

LaVergne, TN USA
16 September 2009
158139LV00004B/20/A